BOLINGBROKE'S

Defence of the Treaty of Utrecht

BOLINGBROKE'S
Defence of the Treaty of Utrecht

BEING

Letters VI–VIII of
The Study & Use of History

With an Introduction by
G. M. TREVELYAN, O.M.

CAMBRIDGE
AT THE UNIVERSITY PRESS
1932

CAMBRIDGE UNIVERSITY PRESS
Cambridge, New York, Melbourne, Madrid, Cape Town,
Singapore, São Paulo, Delhi, Mexico City

Cambridge University Press
The Edinburgh Building, Cambridge CB2 8RU, UK

Published in the United States of America by Cambridge University Press, New York

www.cambridge.org
Information on this title: www.cambridge.org/9781107681538

First published 1932
First paperback edition 2013

A catalogue record for this publication is available from the British Library

ISBN 978-1-107-68153-8 Paperback

CONTENTS

INTRODUCTION

This reprint consists of numbers VI–VIII of Boling-broke's *Letters on the Study and Use of History*. It has been decided not to reprint the first five letters, which are of greatly inferior interest to the modern reader, and only serve to obscure the great merit and importance of Letters VI–VIII. The first five letters are a lengthy argument, served up in a somewhat pedantic and obsolete style, on the value of historical knowledge as the basis of a philo-sophy of human affairs. Of very different interest is the practical illustration of these principles in the portion here printed.

The first dozen pages of Letter VI show the acute and powerful mind of the author generalizing on the causes and character of the Reformation and the rise of the national monarchies, with an insight that even at this day is suggestive and illuminating, and is indeed astonishing if we consider that it was written in 1735–6, before the dawn of modern historical study, before the era of Robertson and Gibbon.

A more detailed account then follows of the rise of the French hegemony in the seventeenth century and the dangers that overshadowed Europe as a consequence.

It will be observed that the author of the Treaty of Utrecht was deeply impressed with the danger of the overgreat power of France during the previous half-century, and the duty of England to maintain the "balance of power" against Louis XIV. Bolingbroke blames Cromwell for not seeing this in the 'fifties; and the Tory

leader calls Charles II's reversal of the Triple Alliance and his
Dover Treaty "equally wicked and impolitic" (pp. 43–44),
an opinion that may profitably be noted nowadays, when
there is some tendency to praise all Charles's actions as indis-
criminately as it was once the fashion to blame them. To
Bolingbroke, William of Orange is the hero of the age, as
he was to his brother Tory, Matthew Prior, another chief
agent in the Treaty of Utrecht.

Bolingbroke praises William III, first because he taught
England to play her proper part in resisting France, and
secondly because of the moderation of his aims and methods
in giving effect to this policy. Bolingbroke, indeed, puts
himself forward as the true heir to William's wise European designs, and there is an important element of truth in
this paradox. In the first place the Tory statesman clears
the ground by admitting that he and his party were wrong
in attacking the Partition Treaties by which at the end of his
reign William tried peacefully to solve the problem of the
Spanish succession by the partition method eventually
followed at Utrecht after a dozen years of war. Bolingbroke also admits that his party was ill-advised at that
period in disarming England by disbanding the army
(pp. 69–70). He goes on to praise William for making a
partition of the Spanish Monarchy the object of the Grand
Alliance of European powers formed in 1701. He points
out that Utrecht carried out the terms of William's Grand
Alliance both in principle and in detail.

In Letter VIII he defends himself as the author of the
Treaty of Utrecht, as carrying out William's original
design of a dozen years before. With this argument goes a
detailed attack on the impractical character of the policy of
Marlborough and the Whigs from 1706 onwards, when,

having won the war, they refused to make peace except on condition of the Austrian Charles being king at Madrid. He shows how they persisted in this design, for years after it had become clear that the Spaniards would not have him, that the military conquest of Spain was impossible, and even after the death of his brother Joseph had made Charles emperor at Vienna. After that, the Allies were in fact fighting to reunite the Spanish and Austrian possessions of Charles V, at the expense of the balance of power in Europe.

In this defence of the general lines of the Tory peace policy of 1710–13, particularly in the matter of Spain, which the Whigs continued for many years to denounce as "infamous," Bolingbroke has, in my opinion, completely made out his case. Macaulay thought so and said so, though Seeley afterwards reiterated the old-fashioned Whig condemnation of Utrecht, for reasons which appear to me too speculative with relation to the later history of the " Family Compact."

One last point of great interest should be noted. On pp. 123–7 Bolingbroke admits that the French power ought to have been further reduced by the terms of peace than it actually was at Utrecht. More fortresses, in his opinion, ought to have been taken from France along the border of the Netherlands—Lille no doubt in particular. Having thus admitted that his work at Utrecht was not wholly satisfactory, Bolingbroke proceeds to defend it as having been the best attainable in the circumstances, owing to the factious conduct of the English Whigs and the European Allies. He argues that these confederates resisted the making of any peace at all, and that therefore the Tory Ministry had to conspire with the French Ministers in the cause of peace against the Allies and the Whig

Opposition. Therefore it was impossible to continue to exert proper pressure on France and extort from her the uttermost fortress. Owing to the conduct of the Allies, peace would not be got at all unless the peace was of a character the French would, in their reduced condition, be glad to accept.

This very remarkable and frank argument of Bolingbroke's ought to be carefully considered by historians before they pronounce upon Utrecht and the proceedings that led up to it, particularly on the withdrawal by the Tory Ministry of the British army from the fighting line. If the argument is not to be swallowed wholesale, neither is it to be rejected with contempt. It is so nice a matter that I have no wish to prejudge it here.

The detachment which enabled Bolingbroke to confess the inadequacy of some of the terms of Utrecht, while defending its main outline particularly as regards the disposal of the Spanish throne, is the detachment of retrospect after more than twenty years. The reader must remember that he is reading the words not of the Henry St John of 1710–12, but of the Bolingbroke of 1735–6, a man chastened by long years of proscription and exile, trying to recover by his pen what he had lost by his actions; a man purged by a long penance of that violent partisanship that had made him, in an hour he never ceased to regret, the Pretender's Secretary. He looks back here upon his former self and his former actions from the standpoint of a political philosophy that was not quite that of Henry St John. With this warning, I commend the admirable pages that follow to the sympathy and judgment of the reader.

G. M. TREVELYAN

August 1932

ON THE STUDY AND USE
OF HISTORY

From what period modern history is peculiarly useful
to the service of our country, viz. From the end of
the fifteenth century to the present. The division of
this into three particular periods: in order to a sketch
of the history and state of Europe from that time.

Since then you are, my lord, by your birth, by the nature
of our government, and by the talents God has given you,
attached for life to the service of your country; since genius
alone cannot enable you to go through this service with
honour to yourself, and advantage to your country;
whether you support, or whether you oppose the administrations that arise; since a great stock of knowledge acquired betimes and continually improved, is necessary to
this end; and since one part of this stock must be collected
from the study of history, as the other part is to be gained
by observation and experience; I come now to speak to
your lordship of such history as has an immediate relation
to the great duty and business of your life, and of the
method to be observed in this study. The notes I have by
me, which were of some little use thus far, serve me no
farther, and I have no books to consult. No matter, I shall
be able to explain my thoughts without their assistance, and
less liable to be tedious. I hope to be as full and as exact on
memory alone, as the manner in which I shall treat the
subject, requires me to be.

I say then, that however closely affairs are linked together
in the progression of governments, and how much soever
events that follow, are dependent on those that precede, the
whole connection diminishes to sight as the chain lengthens;
till at last it seems to be broken, and the links that are continued from that point, bear no proportion nor any simili-
tude to the former. I would not be understood to speak
only of those great changes, that are wrought by a concurrence of extraordinary events; for instance the expulsion of
one nation, the destruction of one government, and the
establishment of another: but even of those that are wrought
in the same governments and among the same people,
slowly and almost imperceptibly, by the necessary effects
of time, and flux condition of human affairs. When such
changes as these happen in several states about the same
time, and consequently affect other states by their vicinity,
and by many different relations which they frequently bear
to one another; this is one of those periods formed, at which
the chain spoken of is so broken as to have little or no real
or visible connection with that which we see continue. A
new situation different from the former, begets new interests in the same proportion of difference; not in this or
that particular state alone, but in all those that are concerned
by vicinity or other relations, as I said just now, in one
general system of policy. New interests beget new maxims
of government, and new methods of conduct. These, in
their turns, beget new manners, new habits, new customs.
The longer this new constitution of affairs continues, the
more will this difference increase: and although some analogy may remain long between what preceded and what
succeeded such a period, yet will this analogy soon become
an object of mere curiosity, not of profitable enquiry. Such

a period therefore is, in the true sense of the words, an epocha or an æra, a point of time at which you stop, or from which you reckon forward. I say forward; because we are not to study in the present case, as chronologers compute backward. Should we persist to carry our researches much higher, and to push them even to some other period of the same kind, we should misemploy our time; the causes then laid having spent themselves, the series of effects derived from them being over, and our concern in both consequently at an end. But a new system of causes and effects, that subsists in our time, and whereof our conduct is to be a part, arising at the last period, and all that passes in our time being dependent on what has passed since that period, or being immediately relative to it, we are extremely concerned to be well informed about all those passages. To be entirely ignorant about the ages that precede this æra would be shameful. Nay some indulgence may be had to a temperate curiosity in the review of them. But to be learned about them is a ridiculous affectation in any man who means to be useful to the present age. Down to this æra let us read history; from this æra, and down to our own time, let us study it.

The end of the fifteenth century seems to be just such a period as I have been describing, for those who live in the eighteenth, and who inhabit the western parts of Europe. A little before, or a little after this point of time, all those events happened, and all those revolutions began, that have produced so vast a change in the manners, customs, and interests of particular nations, and in the whole policy, ecclesiastical and civil, of these parts of the world. I must descend here into some detail, not of histories, collections, or memorials; for all these are well enough known: and though the contents are in the heads of few, the books are in the hands of many. But instead of shewing your lordship where to look, I shall contribute more to your entertainment and instruction, by marking out, as well as my memory will serve me to do it, what you are to look for, and by furnishing a kind of clue to your studies. I shall give, according to custom, the first place to religion.

A view of the ecclesiastical government of Europe from the beginning of the sixteenth century.

Observe then, my lord, that the demolition of the papal throne was not attempted with success till the beginning of the sixteenth century. If you are curious to cast your eyes back, you will find Berenger in the eleventh, who was soon silenced; Arnoldus in the same, who was soon hanged; Valdo in the twelfth, and our Wickliff in the fourteenth, as well as others perhaps whom I do not recollect. Sometimes the doctrines of the church were alone attacked; and sometimes the doctrine, the discipline and the usurpations of the pope. But little fires, kindled in corners of a dark world, were soon stifled by that great abettor of christian unity, the hangman. When they spread and blazed out, as in the case of the Albigeois and of the Hussites, armies were raised to extinguish them by torrents of blood; and such saints as Dominic, with the crucifix in their hands, instigated the troops to the utmost barbarity. Your lordship will find that the church of Rome was maintained by such charitable and salutary means among others, till the period spoken of: and you will be curious, I am sure, to enquire how this period came to be more fatal to her than any former conjuncture. A multitude of circumstances which you will easily trace in the histories of the fifteenth and sixteenth centuries, to go no farther back, concurred to bring about this great event: and a multitude of others as easy to be traced, concurred to hinder the demolition from becoming total, and to prop the tottering fabric. Among these circumstances, there is one less complicated and more obvious than others, which was of principal and universal influence. The art of printing had been invented about forty or fifty years before the period we fix: from that time, the resurrection of letters hastened on apace; and at this period they had made great progress, and were cultivated with great application. Mahomet the second drove them out of the east into the west; and the popes proved worse politicians than the mufties in this respect. Nicholas the fifth encouraged learning, and learned men. Sixtus the fourth was, if I mistake not, a great collector of books at least: and Leo the tenth was the patron of every art and science. The magicians themselves broke the charm by which they had bound mankind for so many ages: and the adventure of that knight-errant, who, thinking himself happy in the arms of a celestial nymph, found that he was the miserable slave of an infernal hag, was in some sort renewed. As soon as the means of acquiring and spreading information grew common, it is no wonder that a system was unravelled, which could not have been woven with success in any ages, but those of gross ignorance, and credulous superstition. I might point out to your lordship many other immediate causes, some general like this that I have mentioned, and some particular. The great schism, for instance, that ended in the beginning of the fifteenth century, and in the Council of Constance, had occasioned prodigious scandal. Two or three vicars of Christ, two or three infallible heads of the church, roaming about the world at a time, furnished matter of ridicule as well as scandal: and whilst they appealed, for so they did in effect, to the laity, and reproached and excommunicated one another, they taught the world what to think of the institution, as well as exercise of the papal authority. The same lesson was taught by the Council of Pisa, that preceded, and by that of Basle, that followed the Council of Constance. The horrid crimes of Alexander the sixth, the saucy ambition of Julius the second, the immense profusion and scandalous exactions of Leo the tenth; all these events and characters, following in a continued series from the beginning of one century, prepared the way for the revolution that happened in the beginning of the next. The state of Germany, the state of England, and that of the North, were particular causes, in these several countries, of this revolution. Such were many remarkable events that happened about the same time, and a little before it, in these and in other nations; and such were likewise the characters of many of the princes of that age, some of whom favoured the reformation like the elector of Saxony, on a principle of conscience; and most of whom favoured it, just as others opposed it, on a principle of interest. This your lordship will discover manifestly to have been the case; and the sole difference you will find between Henry the eighth and Francis the first, one of whom separated from the pope, as the other adhered to him, is this: Henry the eighth divided, with the secular clergy and his people, the spoil of the pope, and his satellites, the monks; Francis the first divided, with the pope, the spoil of his clergy, secular and regular, and of his people. With the same impartial eye that your lordship surveys the abuses of religion, and the corruptions of the church as well as court of Rome, which brought on the reformation at this period; you will observe the characters and conduct of those who began, who propagated, and who favoured the reformation: and from your observation of these, as well as of the unsystematical manner in which it was carried on at the same time in various places, and of the want of concert, nay even of charity, among the reformers, you will learn what to think of the several religions that unite in their opposition to the Roman, and yet hate one another most heartily; what to think of the several sects that have sprouted, like suckers, from the same great roots; and wha the true principles are of protestant ecclesiastical policy This policy had no being till Luther made his establishment in Germany; till Zwinglius began another in Switzerland, which Calvin carried on, and, like Americus Vesputius who followed Christopher Columbus, robbed the first adventurer of his honour; and till the reformation in our country was perfected under Edward the sixth and Elizabeth. Even popish ecclesiastical policy is no longer the same since that æra. His holiness is no longer at the head of the whole western church: and to keep the part that adheres to him, he is obliged to loosen their chains, and to lighten his yoke. The spirit and pretensions of his court are the same, but not the power. He governs by expedient and management more, and by authority less. His decrees and his briefs are in danger of being refused, explained away, or evaded, unless he negociates their acceptance before he gives them, governs in concert with his flock, and feeds his sheep according to their humour and interest. In short, his excommunications, that made the greatest emperors tremble, are despised by the lowest members of his own communion; and the remaining attachment to him has been, from this æra, rather a political expedient to preserve an appearance of unity, than a principle of conscience; whatever some bigotted princes may have thought, whatever ambitious prelates and hireling scribblers may have taught, and whatever a people, worked up to enthusiasm by fanatical preachers, may have acted. Proofs of this would be easy to draw, not only from the conduct of such princes, as Ferdinand the first, and Maximilian the second, who could scarce be esteemed papists, though they continued in the pope's communion: but even from that of princes who persecuted their protestant subjects with great violence. Enough has been said, I think, to shew your lordship how little need there is of going up higher than the beginning of the sixteenth century in the study of history, to acquire all the knowledge necessary at this time in ecclesiastical policy, or in civil policy as far as it is relative to this. Historical monuments of this sort are in every man's hand, the facts are sufficiently verified, and the entire scenes lie open to our observation: even that scene of solemn refined banter exhibited in the Council of Trent, imposes on no man who reads Paolo, as well as Pallavicini, and the letters of Vargas.

A view of the civil government of Europe in the beginning of the sixteenth century.

I. IN FRANCE

A very little higher need we go, to observe those great changes in the civil constitutions of the principal nations of Europe, in the partition of power among them, and by consequence in the whole system of European policy, which have operated so strongly for more than two centuries, and which operate still. I will not affront the memory of our Henry the seventh so much as to compare him to Lewis the eleventh: and yet I perceive some resemblance between them; which would perhaps appear greater if Philip of Commines had wrote the history of Henry as well as that of Lewis; or if my lord Bacon had wrote that of Lewis as well as that of Henry. This prince came to the crown of England a little before the close of the fifteenth century: and Lewis began his reign in France about twenty years sooner. These reigns make remarkable periods in the histories of both nations. To reduce the power, privileges, and possessions of the nobility, and to increase the wealth and authority of the crown, was the principal object of both. In this their success was so great, that the constitutions of the two governments have had, since that time, more resemblance, in name and in form, than in reality, to the constitutions that prevailed before. Lewis the eleventh was the first, say the French, "qui mit les rois hors de page." The independency of the nobility had rendered the state of his predecessors very dependent, and their power precarious. They were the sovereigns of great vassals; but these vassals were so powerful, that one of them was sometimes able, and two or three of them always to give law to the sovereign. Before Lewis came to the crown, the English had been driven out of their possessions in France, by the poor character of Henry the sixth, the domestic troubles of his reign, and the defection of the house of Burgundy from his alliance, much more than by the ability of Charles the seventh, who seems to have been neither a greater hero nor a greater politician than Henry the sixth; and even then by the vigour and union of the French nobility in his service. After Lewis came to the crown, Edward the fourth made a shew of carrying the war again into France: but he soon returned home, and your lordship will not be at a loss to find much better reasons for his doing so, in the situation of his affairs

and the characters of his allies, than those which Philip of
Commines draws from the artifice of Lewis, from his good
cheer, and his pensions. Now from this time our pretensions
on France were in effect given up: and Charles the bold,
the last prince of the house of Burgundy, being killed,
Lewis had no vassal able to molest him. He re-united the
duchy of Burgundy and Artois to his crown, he acquired
Provence by gift, and his son Britany by marriage: and
thus France grew, in the course of a few years, into that
great and compact body which we behold at this time. The
history of France before this period, is like that of Germany,
a complicated history of several states and several interests;
sometimes concurring like members of the same monarchy,
and sometimes warring on one another. Since this period,
the history of France is the history of one state under a
more uniform and orderly government; the history of a
monarchy wherein the prince is possessor of some, as well
as lord of all the great fieffees: and the authority of many
tyrants centering in one, though the people are not become
more free, yet the whole system of domestic policy is entirely changed. Peace at home is better secured, and the
nation grown fitter to carry war abroad. The governors of
great provinces and of strong fortresses have opposed their
king, and taken arms against his authority and commission
since that time: but yet there is no more resemblance between the authority and pretensions of these governors, or
the nature and occasions of these disputes, and the authority
and pretensions of the vassals of the crown in former days,
or the nature and occasions of their disputes with the prince
and with one another, than there is between the ancient and
the present peers of France. In a word, the constitution is
so altered, that any knowledge we can acquire about it, in

the history that precedes this period, will serve to little
purpose in our study of the history that follows it, and to
less purpose still in assisting us to judge of what passes in
the present age. The kings of France since that time, more
masters at home, have been able to exert themselves more
abroad: and they began to do so immediately; for Charles
the eighth, son and successor of Lewis the eleventh, formed
great designs of foreign conquests, though they were disappointed by his inability, by the levity of the nation, and
by other causes. Lewis the twelfth and Francis the first,
but especially Francis, meddled deep in the affairs of Europe:
and though the superior genius of Ferdinand called the
catholic, and the star of Charles the fifth prevailed against
them, yet the efforts they made, shew sufficiently how the
strength and importance of this monarchy were increased
in their time. From whence we may date likewise the rivalship of the house of France, for we may reckon that of
Valois and that of Bourbon as one upon this occasion, and
the house of Austria; that continues at this day, and that
has cost so much blood and so much treasure in the course
of it.

II. IN ENGLAND

Though the power and influence of the nobility sunk in the
great change that began under Henry the seventh in England, as they did in that which began under Lewis the
eleventh in France; yet the new constitutions that these
changes produced were very different. In France the lords
alone lost, the king alone gained; the clergy held their possessions and their immunities, and the people remained in a
state of mitigated slavery. But in England the people gained
as well as the crown. The commons had already a share in

the legislature; so that the power and influence of the lords being broke by Henry the seventh, and the property of the commons increasing by the sale that his son made of church lands, the power of the latter increased of course by this change in a constitution, the forms whereof were favourable to them. The union of the roses put an end to the civil wars of York and Lancaster, that had succeeded those we commonly call the barons' wars, and the humour of warring in France, that had lasted near four hundred years under the Normans and Plantagenets, for plunder as well as conquest was spent. Our temple of Janus was shut by Henry the seventh. We neither laid waste our own nor other countries any longer: and wise laws and a wise government changed insensibly the manners, and gave a new turn to the spirit of our people. We were no longer the free-booters we had been. Our nation maintained her reputation in arms whenever the public interest or the public authority required it; but war ceased to be, what it had been, our principal and almost our sole profession. The arts of peace prevailed among us. We became husbandmen, manufacturers and merchants, and we emulated neighbouring nations in literature. It is from this time that we ought to study the history of our country, my lord, with the utmost application. We are not much concerned to know with critical accuracy what were the ancient forms of our parliaments, concerning which, however, there is little room for dispute from the reign of Henry the third at least; nor in short the whole system of our civil constitution before Henry the seventh, and of our ecclesiastical constitution before Henry the eighth. But he who has not studied and acquired a thorough knowledge of them both, from these periods down to the present time, in all the variety of events by which they have been affected, will be very unfit to judge or to take care of either. Just as little are we concerned to know, in any nice detail, what the conduct of our princes, relatively to their neighbours on the continent, was before this period, and at a time when the partition of power and a multitude of other circumstances rendered the whole political system of Europe, so vastly different from that which has existed since. But he who has not traced this conduct from the period we fix, down to the present age, wants a principal part of the knowledge that every English minister of state should have. Ignorance in the respects here spoken of is the less pardonable, because we have more and more authentic means of information concerning this, than concerning any other period. Anecdotes enough to glut the curiosity of some persons, and to silence all the captious cavils of others, will never be furnished by any portion of history; nor indeed can they according to the nature and course of human affairs: but he who is content to read and observe, like a senator and a statesman, will find in our own and in foreign historians as much information as he wants, concerning the affairs of our island, her fortune at home, and her conduct abroad, from the fifteenth century to the eighteenth. I refer to foreign historians, as well as to our own, for this series of our own history; not only because it is reasonable to see in what manner the historians of other countries have related the transactions wherein we have been concerned, and what judgment they have made of our conduct, domestic and foreign, but for another reason likewise. Our nation has furnished as ample and as important matter, good and bad, for history, as any nation under the sun: and yet we must yield the palm in writing history most certainly to the Italians and to the French, and, I fear, even to the Germans. The only two pieces of history we have, in any respect to be compared with the ancient, are, the reign of Henry the seventh by my lord Bacon, and the History of our civil war in the last century by your noble ancestor my lord chancellor Clarendon. But we have no general history to be compared with some of other countries: neither have we, which I lament much more, particular histories, except the two I have mentioned, nor writers of memorials nor collectors of monuments and anecdotes, to vie in number or in merit with those that foreign nations can boast; from Commines, Guicciardin, Du Bellay, Paolo, Davila, Thuanus, and a multitude of others, down through the whole period that I propose to your lordship. But although this be true, to our shame; yet it is true likewise that we want no necessary means of information. They lie open to our industry, and our discernment. Foreign writers are for the most part scarce worth reading when they speak of our domestic affairs: nor are our English writers for the most part of greater value when they speak of foreign affairs. In this mutual defect, the writers of other countries are, I think, more excusable than ours: for the nature of our government, the political principles in which we are bred, our distinct interests as islanders, and the complicated various interests and humours of our parties, all these are so peculiar to ourselves, and so different from the notions, manners, and habits of other nations, that it is not wonderful they should be puzzled or should fall into error, when they undertake to give relations of events that result from all these, or to pass any judgment upon them. But as these historians are mutually defective, so they mutually supply each other's defects. We must compare them therefore, make use of our discernment, and draw our conclusions from both. If we proceed in this manner, we have an ample fund of history in our power, from whence to collect sufficient authentic information; and we must proceed in this manner, even with our own historians of different religions, sects, and parties, or run the risk of being misled by domestic ignorance and prejudice in this case, as well as by foreign ignorance and prejudice in the other.

III. IN SPAIN AND THE EMPIRE

Spain figured little in Europe till the latter part of the fifteenth century: till Castile and Arragon were united by the marriage of Ferdinand and Isabella; till the total expulsion of the Moors, and till the discovery of the West Indies. After this, not only Spain took a new form, and grew into immense power; but the heir of Ferdinand and Isabella being heir likewise of the houses of Burgundy and Austria, such an extent of dominion accrued to him by all these successions, and such an addition of rank and authority by his election to the empire, as no prince had been master of in Europe from the days of Charles the great. It is proper to observe here how the policy of the Germans altered in the choice of an emperor, because the effects of this alteration have been great. When Rodolphus of Hapsburgh was chose in the year one thousand two hundred and seventy, or about that time, the poverty and the low estate of this prince, who had been marshal of the court to a king of Bohemia, was an inducement to elect him. The disorderly and lawless state of the empire made the princes of it in those days unwilling to have a more powerful head. But a contrary maxim took place at this æra: Charles the fifth and Francis the first, the two most powerful princes of Europe, were the sole candidates; for the elector of Saxony, who is

said to have declined, was rather unable to stand in com-
petition with them: and Charles was chosen by the unani-
mous suffrages of the electoral college if I mistake not.
Another Charles, Charles the fourth, who was made emperor illegally enough on the deposition of Lewis of Bavaria,
and about one hundred and fifty years before, seems to me
to have contributed doubly to establish this maxim; by the
wise constitutions that he procured to pass, that united the
empire in a more orderly form and better system of government; and by alienating the imperial revenues to such a
degree, that they were no longer sufficient to support an
emperor who had not great revenues of his own. The same
maxim and other circumstances have concurred to keep the
empire in this family ever since, as it had been often before;
and this family having large dominions in the empire, and
larger pretensions, as well as dominions, out of it, the other
states of Europe, France, Spain, and England particularly,
have been more concerned since this period in the affairs of
Germany, than they were before it: and by consequence
the history of Germany, from the beginning of the sixteenth
century, is of importance, and a necessary part of that knowledge which your lordship desires to acquire.

The Dutch commonwealth was not formed till near a
century later. But as soon as it was formed, nay even
whilst it was forming, these provinces, that were lost to
observation among the many that composed the dominions
of Burgundy and Austria, became so considerable a part of
the political system of Europe, that their history must be
studied by every man who would inform himself of this
system.

Soon after this state had taken being, others of a more
ancient original began to mingle in those disputes and wars,

those councils, negociations, and treaties, that are to be the principal objects of your lordship's application in the study of history. That of the northern crowns deserves your attention little, before the last century. Till the election of Frederick the first to the crown of Denmark, and till that wonderful revolution which the first Gustavus brought about in Sweden, it is nothing more than a confused rhapsody of events, in which the great kingdoms and states of Europe neither had any concern, nor took any part. From the time I have mentioned the northern crowns have turned their councils and their arms often southwards, and Sweden particularly, with prodigious effect.

To what purpose should I trouble your lordship with the mention of histories of other nations? they are either such as have no relation to the knowledge you would acquire, like that of the Poles, the Muscovites, or the Turks; or they are such as having an occasional or a secondary relation to it, fall of course into your scheme; like the history of Italy for instance, which is sometimes a part of that of France, sometimes of that of Spain, and sometimes of that of Germany. The thread of history, that you are to keep, is that of the nations who are, and must always be concerned in the same scenes of action with your own. These are the principal nations of the west. Things that have no immediate relation to your own country, or to them, are either too remote, or too minute, to employ much of your time: and their history and your own is, for all your purposes, the whole history of Europe.

The two great powers, that of France and that of Austria, being formed, and a rivalship established by consequence between them; it began to be the interest of their neighbours to oppose the strongest and most enterprising of the two, and to be the ally and friend of the weakest. From hence arose the notion of a balance of power in Europe, on the equal poize of which the safety and tranquillity of all must depend. To destroy the equality of this balance has been the aim of each of these rivals in his turn: and to hinder it from being destroyed, by preventing too much power from falling into one scale, has been the principle of all the wise councils of Europe, relative to France and to the house of Austria, through the whole period that began at the æra we have fixed, and subsists at this hour. To make a careful and just observation, therefore, of the rise and decline of these powers, in the two last centuries and in the present; of the projects which their ambition formed; of the means they employed to carry these projects on with success; of the means employed by others to defeat them; of the issue of all these endeavours in war and in negociation; and particularly, to bring your observations home to your own country and your own use, of the conduct that England held, to her honour or dishonour, to her advantage or disadvantage, in every one of the numerous and important conjunctures that happened—ought to be the principal subject of your lordship's attention in reading and reflecting on this part of modern history.

Now to this purpose you will find it of great use, my lord, when you have a general plan of the history in your mind, to go over the whole again in another method; which I propose to be this. Divide the entire period into such particular periods as the general course of affairs will mark out to you sufficiently, by the rise of new conjunctures, of different schemes of conduct, and of different theatres of action. Examine this period of history as you would examine a tragedy or a comedy; that is, take first the idea or a

general notion of the whole, and after that examine every
act and every scene apart. Consider them in themselves,
and consider them relatively to one another. Read this
history as you would that of any ancient period; but study
it afterwards, as it would not be worth your while to study
the other; nay as you could not have it in your power the
means of studying the other, if the study was really worth
your while. The former part of this period abounds in great
historians: and the latter part is so modern, that even tradition is authentic enough to supply the want of good
history, if we are curious to enquire, and if we hearken to
the living with the same impartiality and freedom of judgment as we read the dead: and he that does one will do the
other. The whole period abounds in memorials, in collections of public acts and monuments of private letters, and
of treaties. All these must come into your plan of study, my
lord; many not to be read through, but all to be consulted
and compared. They must not lead you, I think, to your
enquiries, but your enquiries must lead you to them. By
joining history and that which we call the materia historica
together in this manner, and by drawing your information
from both, your lordship will acquire not only that knowledge, which many have in some degree, of the great transactions that have passed, and the great events that have
happened in Europe during this period, and of their immediate and obvious causes and consequences; but your
lordship will acquire a much superior knowledge, and such
a one as very few men possess almost in any degree, a knowledge of the true political system of Europe during this time.
You will see it in it's primitive principles, in the constitutions
of governments, the situations of countries, their national and
true interests, the characters and the religion of people, and

2-2

other permanent circumstances. You will trace it through all its fluctuations, and observe how the objects vary seldom, but the means perpetually, according to the different characters of princes and of those who govern; the different abilities of those who serve; the course of accidents, and a multitude of other irregular and contingent circumstances.

The particular periods into which the whole period should be divided, in my opinion, are these. 1. From the fifteenth to the end of the sixteenth century. 2. From thence to the Pyrenean treaty. 3. From thence down to the present time.

Your lordship will find this division as apt and as proper, relatively to the particular histories of England, France, Spain, and Germany, the principal nations concerned, as it is relatively to the general history of Europe.

The death of Queen Elizabeth, and the accession of king James the first, made a vast alteration in the government of our nation at home, and in her conduct abroad, about the end of the first of these periods. The wars that religion occasioned, and ambition fomented in France, through the reigns of Francis the second, Charles the ninth, Henry the third, and a part of Henry the fourth, ended: and the furies of the league were crushed by this great prince, about the same time. Philip the second of Spain marks this period likewise by his death, and by the exhausted condition in which he left the monarchy he governed: which took the lead no longer in disturbing the peace of mankind, but acted a second part in abetting the bigotry and ambition of Ferdinand the second and the third. The thirty years war that devastated Germany did not begin till the eighteenth year of the seventeenth century, but the seeds of it were sowing some time before, and even at the end of the sixteenth. Ferdinand the first and Maximilian had shewn much lenity and moderation in the disputes and troubles that arose on account of religion. Under Rodolphus and Matthias, as the succession of their cousin Ferdinand approached, the fires that were covered began to smoke and to sparkle; and if the war did not begin with this century, the preparation for it, and the expectation of it did.

The second period ends in one thousand six hundred and sixty, the year of the restoration of Charles the second to the throne of England; when our civil wars, and all the disorders which Cromwell's usurpation had produced, were over: and therefore a remarkable point of time, with respect to our country. It is no less remarkable with respect to Germany, Spain, and France.

As to Germany; the ambitious projects of the German branch of Austria had been entirely defeated, the peace of the empire had been restored, and almost a new constitution formed, or an old one revived, by the treaties of Westphalia; nay the imperial eagle was not only fallen, but her wings were clipped.

As to Spain; the Spanish branch was fallen as low twelve years afterwards, that is, in the year one thousand six hundred and sixty. Philip the second left his successors a ruined monarchy. He left them something worse; he left them his example and his principles of government, founded in ambition, in pride, in ignorance, in bigotry, and all the pedantry of state. I have read somewhere or other, that the war of the Low Countries alone cost him, by his own confession, five hundred and sixty-four millions, a prodigious sum in what species soever he reckoned. Philip the third and Philip the fourth followed his example and his principles of government, at home and abroad. At home, there

was much form, but no good order, no œconomy, nor
wisdom of policy in the state. The church continued to
devour the state, and that monster the inquisition to dis-
people the country, even more than perpetual war, and all
the numerous colonies that Spain had sent to the West
Indies: for your lordship will find that Philip the third drove
more than nine hundred thousand Moriscoes out of his
dominions by one edict, with such circumstances of inhumanity in the execution of it, as Spaniards alone could
exercise, and that tribunal who had provoked this unhappy
race to revolt, could alone approve. Abroad, the conduct
of these princes was directed by the same wild spirit of
ambition: rash in undertaking, though slow to execute, and
obstinate in pursuing, though unable to succeed, they opened
a new sluice to let out the little life and vigour that remained
in their monarchy. Philip the second is said to have been
piqued against his uncle Ferdinand, for refusing to yield the
empire to him on the abdication of Charles the fifth. Certain
it is, that as much as he loved to disturb the peace of mankind, and to meddle in every quarrel that had the appearance
of supporting the Roman and oppressing every other church,
he meddled little in the affairs of Germany. But, Ferdinand
and Maximilian dead, and the offspring of Maximilian ex-
tinct, the kings of Spain espoused the interests of the other
branch of their family, entertained remote views of ambition in favour of their own branch, even on that side, and
made all the enterprizes of Ferdinand of Gratz, both before
and after his elevation to the empire, the common cause of
the house of Austria. What compleated their ruin was this,
they knew not how to lose, nor when to yield. They acknowledged the independency of the Dutch commonwealth, and became the allies of their ancient subjects, at

the treaty of Munster: but they would not forego their usurped claim on Portugal, and they persisted to carry on singly the war against France. Thus they were reduced to such a lowness of power as can hardly be paralleled in any other case: and Philip the fourth was obliged at last to conclude a peace, on terms repugnant to his inclination, to that of his people, to the interest of Spain, and to that of all Europe, in the Pyrenean treaty.

As to France; this æra of the entire fall of the Spanish power is likewise that from which we may reckon that France grew as formidable, as we have seen her, to her neighbours, in power and pretensions. Henry the fourth meditated great designs, and prepared to act a great part in Europe in the very beginning of this period, when Ravaillac stabbed him. His designs died with him, and are rather guessed at than known; for surely those which his historian Perefixe, and the compilers of Sully's memorials ascribe to him, of a christian commonwealth divided into fifteen states, and of a senate to decide all differences, and to maintain this new constitution of Europe, are too chimerical to have been really his: but his general design of abasing the house of Austria, and establishing the superior power in that of Bourbon, was taken up about twenty years after his death, by Richelieu, and was pursued by him and by Mazarin with so much ability and success, that it was effected entirely by the treaties of Westphalia, and by the Pyrenean treaty: that is, at the end of the second of those periods I have presumed to propose to your lordship.

When the third, in which we now are, will end, and what circumstances will mark the end of it, I know not: but this I know, that the great events and revolutions, which have happened in the course of it, interest us still more nearly than those of the two precedent periods. I intended to have drawn up an elenchus or summary of the three, but I doubted, on further reflection, whether my memory would enable me to do it with exactness enough: and I saw that, if I was able to do it, the deduction would be immeasurably long. Something of this kind however it may be reasonable to attempt, in speaking of the last period: which may here-after occasion a further trouble to your lordship.

But to give you some breathing time, I will postpone it at present, and am in the mean while,

My Lord,

Your, &c.

A sketch of the state and history of Europe, from the Pyrenean treaty in one thousand six hundred and fifty-nine, to the year one thousand six hundred and eighty-eight.

The first observation I shall make on this third period of modern history is, that as the ambition of Charles the fifth, who united the whole formidable power of Austria in himself, and the restless temper, the cruelty, and bigotry of Philip the second, were principally objects of the attention and solicitude of the councils of Europe, in the first of these periods; and as the ambition of Ferdinand the second, and the third, who aimed at nothing less than extirpating the protestant interest, and under that pretence subduing the liberties of Germany, were objects of the same kind in the second; so an opposition to the growing power of France, or to speak more properly, to the exorbitant ambition of the house of Bourbon, has been the principal affair of Europe, during the greatest part of the present period. The design of aspiring to universal monarchy, was imputed to Charles the fifth, as soon as he began to give proofs of his ambition and capacity. The same design was imputed to Lewis the fourteenth, as soon as he began to feel his own strength, and the weakness of his neighbours. Neither of these princes was induced, I believe, by the flattery of his courtiers, or the apprehensions of his adversaries, to entertain so chimerical a design as this would have been, even in that false sense wherein the word universal is so often understood: and I mistake very much if either of them was of a character, or in circumstances, to undertake it. Both of them had strong desires to raise their families higher, and to extend their dominions farther; but neither of them had that bold and adventurous ambition which makes a conqueror and an hero. These apprehensions however, were given wisely, and taken usefully. They cannot be given nor taken too soon when such powers as these arise; because when such powers as these are besieged as it were early, by the common policy and watchfulness of their neighbours, each of them may in his turn of strength sally forth, and gain a little ground; but none of them will be able to push their conquests far, and much less to consummate the entire projects of their ambition. Besides the occasional opposition that was given to Charles the fifth, by our Henry the eighth, according to the different moods of humour he was in; by the popes, according to the several turns of their private interest, and by the princes of Germany according to the occasions or pretences that religion or civil liberty furnished, he had from his first setting out a rival and an enemy in Francis the first, who did not maintain his cause "in forma pauperis," if I may use such an expression: as we have seen the house of Austria, sue, in our days, for dominion, at the gate of every palace in Europe. Francis the first was the principal in his own quarrels, paid his own armies, fought his own battles; and though his valour alone did not hinder Charles the fifth from subduing all Europe, as Bayle, a better philologer than politician, somewhere asserts, but a multitude of other circumstances easily to be traced in history; yet he contributed by his victories, and even by his defeats, to waste the strength and check the course of that growing power. Lewis the fourteenth had no rival of this kind in the house of

Austria, nor indeed any enemy of this importance to com-
bat, till the prince of Orange became king of Great Britain:
and he had great advantages in many other respects, which
it is necessary to consider, in order to make a true judgment
on the affairs of Europe from the year one thousand six
hundred and sixty. You will discover the first of these
advantages, and such as were productive of all the rest, in
the conduct of Richelieu and of Mazarin. Richelieu formed
the great design, and laid the foundations: Mazarin pursued
the design, and raised the superstructure. If I do not
deceive myself extremely, there are few passages in history
that deserve your lordship's attention more than the
conduct that the first and greatest of these ministers held,
in laying the foundations I speak of. You will observe how
he helped to embroil affairs on every side, and to keep the
house of Austria at bay as it were; how he entered into the
quarrels of Italy against Spain, into that concerning the
Valteline, and that concerning the succession of Mantua:
without engaging so deep as to divert him from another
great object of his policy, subduing Rochelle and disarming
the Huguenots. You will observe how he turned himself,
after this was done, to stop the progress of Ferdinand in
Germany. Whilst Spain fomented discontents in the court,
and disorders in the kingdom of France by all possible
means, even by taking engagements with the duke of
Rohan, and for supporting the protestants; Richelieu
abetted the same interest in Germany against Ferdinand;
and in the Low Countries against Spain. The emperor was
become almost the master in Germany. Christian the fourth,
king of Denmark, had been at the head of a league, wherein
the United provinces, Sweden, and Lower Saxony entered
to oppose his progress: but Christian had been defeated by

Tilly and Valstein, and obliged to conclude a treaty at Lubec, where Ferdinand gave him the law. It was then that Gustavus Adolphus, with whom Richelieu made an alliance, entered into this war, and soon turned the fortune of it. The French minister had not yet engaged his master openly in the war; but when the Dutch grew impatient, and threatened to renew their truce with Spain, unless France declared; when the king of Sweden was killed, and the battle of Nordlingen lost; when Saxony had turned again to the side of the emperor, and Brandenburg, and so many others had followed this example, that Hesse almost alone persisted in the Swedish alliance; then Richelieu engaged his master, and profited of every circumstance which the conjuncture afforded, to engage him with advantage. For, first, he had a double advantage by engaging so late: that of coming fresh into the quarrel against a wearied and almost exhausted enemy: and that of yielding to the impatience of his friends, who, pressed by their necessities and by the want they had of France, gave this minister an opportunity of laying those claims, and establishing those pretensions, in all his treaties with Holland, Sweden, and the princes and states of the empire, on which he had projected the future aggrandisement of France. The manner in which he engaged, and the air that he gave to his engagement, were advantages of the second sort, advantages of reputation and credit; yet were these of no small moment in the course of the war, and operated strongly in favour of France, as he designed they should, even after his death, and at and after the treaties of Westphalia. He varnished ambition with the most plausible and popular pretences. The elector of Treves had put himself under the protection of France: and, if I remember right, he made this step when the emperor could not protect him against the Swedes, whom he had reason to apprehend. No matter, the governor of Luxemburg was ordered to surprise Treves, and to seize the elector. He executed his orders with success, and carried this prince prisoner into Brabant. Richelieu seized the lucky circumstance; he reclaimed the elector: and on the refusal of the cardinal infant, the war was declared. France, you see, appeared the common friend of liberty, the defender of it in the Low Countries against the king of Spain, and in Germany against the emperor, as well as the protector of the princes of the empire, many of whose estates had been illegally invaded, and whose persons were no longer safe from violence even in their own palaces. All these appearances were kept up in the negociations at Munster, where Mazarin reaped what Richelieu had sowed. The demands that France made for herself were very great; but the conjuncture was favourable, and she improved it to the utmost. No figure could be more flattering than her's, at the head of these negociations; nor more mortifying than the emperor's, through the whole course of the treaty. The princes and states of the empire had been treated as vassals by the emperor: France determined then to treat with him on this occasion as sovereigns, and supported them in this determination. Whilst Sweden seemed concerned for the protestant interest alone, and shewed no other regard, as she had no other alliance; France affected to be impartial alike to the protestant and to the papist, and to have no interest at heart but the common interest of the Germanic body. Her demands were excessive, but they were to be satisfied principally out of the emperor's patrimonial dominions. It had been the art of her ministers to establish this general maxim on many particular experiences, that the

grandeur of France was a real, and would be a constant
security to the rights and liberties of the empire against the
emperor; and it is no wonder therefore, this maxim pre-
vailing, injuries, resentments, and jealousies being fresh on
one side, and services, obligations, and confidence on the
other, that the Germans were not unwilling France should
extend her empire on this side of the Rhine, whilst Sweden
did the same on this side of the Baltic. These treaties, and the
immense credit and influence that France had acquired by
them in the empire, put it out of the power of one branch of
the house of Austria to return the obligations of assistance
to the other, in the war that continued between France and
Spain, till the Pyrenean treaty. By this treaty the superiority
of the house of Bourbon over the house of Austria was not
only compleated and confirmed, but the great design of
uniting the Spanish and the French monarchies under the
former was laid.

The third period therefore begins by a great change of
the balance of power in Europe, and by the prospect of one
much greater and more fatal. Before I descend into the
particulars I intend to mention, of the course of affairs, and
of the political conduct of the great powers of Europe in
this third period; give me leave to cast my eyes once more
back on the second. The reflection I am going to make
seems to me important, and leads to all that is to follow.

The Dutch made their peace separately at Munster with
Spain, who acknowledged them the sovereignty and independency of their commonwealth. The French, who had
been, after our Elizabeth, their principal support, reproached
them severely for this breach of faith. They excused themselves in the best manner, and by the best reasons, they
could. All this your lordship will find in the monu-

ments of that time. But I think it not improbable that they had a motive you will not find there, and which it was not proper to give as a reason or excuse to the French. Might not the wise men amongst them consider even then, besides the immediate advantages that accrued by this treaty to their commonwealth, that the imperial power was fallen; that the power of Spain was vastly reduced; that the house of Austria was nothing more than the shadow of a great name, and that the house of Bourbon was advancing, by large strides, to a degree of power as exorbitant, and as formidable as that of the other family had been in the hands of Charles the fifth, of Philip the second, and lately of the two Ferdinands? might they not foresee, even then, what happened in the course of very few years, when they were obliged, for their own security, to assist their old enemies the Spaniards against their old friends the French? I think they might. Our Charles the first was no great politician, and yet he seemed to discern that the balance of power was turning in favour of France, some years before the treaties of Westphalia. He refused to be neuter, and threatened to take part with Spain, if the French pursued the design of besieging Dunkirk and Graveline, according to a concert taken between them and the Dutch, and in pursuance of a treaty for dividing the Spanish Low Countries, which Richelieu had negociated. Cromwell either did not discern this turn of the balance of power, long afterwards when it was much more visible; or, discerning it, he was induced by reasons of private interest to act against the general interest of Europe. Cromwell joined with France against Spain, and though he got Jamaica and Dunkirk, he drove the Spaniards into a necessity of making a peace with France, that has disturbed the peace of the world almost fourscore years, and the consequences of which have well-nigh beggared in our times the nation he enslaved in his. There is a tradition, I have heard it from persons who lived in those days, and I believe it came from Thurloe, that Cromwell was in treaty with Spain, and ready to turn his arms against France when he died. If this fact was certain, as little as I honour his memory, I should have some regret that he died so soon. But whatever his intentions were, we must charge the Pyrenean treaty, and the fatal consequences of it, in a great measure to his account. The Spaniards abhorred the thought of marrying their Infanta to Lewis the fourteenth. It was on this point that they broke the negociation Lionne had begun: and your lordship will perceive, that if they resumed it afterwards, and offered the marriage they had before rejected, Cromwell's league with France was a principal inducement to this alteration of their resolutions.

The precise point at which the scales of power turn like that of the solstice in either tropic, is imperceptible to common observation: and, in one case as in the other, some progress must be made in the new direction, before the change is perceived. They who are in the sinking scale, for in the political balance of power, unlike to all others, the scale that is empty sinks, and that which is full rises; they who are in the sinking scale do not easily come off from the habitual prejudices of superior wealth, or power, or skill, or courage, nor from the confidence that these prejudices inspire. They who are in the rising scale do not immediately feel their strength, nor assume that confidence in it which successful experience gives them afterwards. They who are the most concerned to watch the variations of this balance, mis-judge often in the same manner, and from the same

prejudices. They continue to dread a power no longer able
to hurt them, or they continue to have no apprehensions of
a power that grows daily more formidable. Spain verified
the first observation at the end of the second period, when,
proud and poor, and enterprizing and feeble, she still
thought herself a match for France. France verified the
second observation at the beginning of the third period,
when the triple alliance stopped the progress of her arms,
which alliances much more considerable were not able to
effect afterwards. The other principal powers of Europe,
in their turns, have verified the third observation in both it's
parts, through the whole course of this period.

When Lewis the fourteenth took the administration of
affairs into his own hands, about the year one thousand six
hundred and sixty, he was in the prime of his age, and had,
what princes seldom have, the advantages of youth and
those of experience together. Their education is generally
bad; for which reason royal birth, that gives a right to the
throne among other people, gave an absolute exclusion
from it among the Mamalukes. His was, in all respects,
except one, as bad as that of other princes. He jested sometimes on his own ignorance; and there were other defects in
his character, owing to his education, which he did not see.
But Mazarin had initiated him betimes into the mysteries of
his policy. He had seen a great part of those foundations
laid, on which he was to raise the fabric of his future grandeur: and as Mazarin finished the work that Richelieu
began, he had the lessons of one, and the examples of both,
to instruct him. He had acquired habits of secrecy and
method, in business; of reserve, discretion, decency, and
dignity, in behaviour. If he was not the greatest king, he
was the best actor of majesty at least, that ever filled a

throne. He by no means wanted that courage which is commonly called bravery, though the want of it was imputed to him in the midst of his greatest triumphs: nor that other courage, less ostentatious and more rarely found, calm, steady, persevering resolution: which seems to arise less from the temper of the body, and is therefore called courage of the mind. He had them both most certainly, and I could produce unquestionable anecdotes in proof. He was, in one word, much superior to any prince with whom he had to do, when he began to govern. He was surrounded with great captains bred in former wars, and with great ministers bred in the same school as himself. They who had worked under Mazarin, worked on the same plan under him; and as they had the advantage of genius, and experience over most of the ministers of other countries, so they had another advantage over those who were equal or superior to them: the advantage of serving a master whose absolute power was established; and the advantage of a situation wherein they might exert their whole capacity without contradiction; over that, for instance, wherein your lordship's great grandfather [Clarendon] was placed, at the same time, in England, and John de Wit in Holland. Among these ministers, Colbert must be mentioned particularly upon this occasion; because it was he who improved the wealth, and consequently the power of France extremely, by the order he put into the finances, and by the encouragement he gave to trade and manufactures. The soil, the climate, the situation of France, the ingenuity, the industry, the vivacity of her inhabitants are such; she has so little want of the product of other countries, and other countries have so many real or imaginary wants to be supplied by her; that when she is not at war with all her neighbours, when her domestic quiet is preserved, and any tolerable administration of government prevails, she must grow rich at the expence of those who trade, and even of those who do not open a trade, with her. Her bawbles, her modes, the follies and extravagancies of her luxury, cost England, about the time we are speaking of, little less than eight hundred thousand pounds sterling a year, and other nations in their proportions. Colbert made the most of all these advantageous circumstances, and whilst he filled the national spunge, he taught his successors how to squeeze it; a secret that he repented having discovered, they say, when he saw the immense sums that were necessary to supply the growing magnificence of his master.

This was the character of Lewis the fourteenth, and this was the state of his kingdom at the beginning of the present period. If his power was great, his pretensions were still greater. He had renounced, and the Infanta with his consent had renounced, all right to the succession of Spain, in the strongest terms that the precaution of the councils of Madrid could contrive. No matter; he consented to these renunciations, but your lordship will find by the letters of Mazarin, and by other memorials, that he acted on the contrary principle, from the first, which he avowed soon afterwards. Such a power, and such pretensions should have given, one would think, an immediate alarm to the rest of Europe. Philip the fourth was broken and decayed, like the monarchy he governed. One of his sons died, as I remember, during the negociations that preceded the year one thousand six hundred and sixty: and the survivor, who was Charles the second, rather languished, than lived, from the cradle to the grave. So dangerous a contingency therefore, as the union of the two monarchies of France and

Spain, being in view forty years together; one would imagine that the principal powers of Europe had the means of preventing it constantly in view during the same time. But it was otherwise. France acted very systematically from the year one thousand six hundred and sixty, to the death of king Charles the second of Spain. She never lost sight of her great object, the succession to the whole Spanish monarchy; and she accepted the will of the king of Spain in favour of the duke of Anjou. As she never lost sight of her great object during this time, so she lost no opportunity of increasing her power, while she waited for that of succeeding in her pretensions. The two branches of Austria were in no condition of making a considerable opposition to her designs and attempts. Holland, who of all other powers was the most concerned to oppose them, was at that time under two influences that hindered her from pursuing her true interest. Her true interest was to have used her utmost endeavours to unite closely and intimately with England on the restoration of king Charles. She did the very contrary. John de Wit, at the head of the Louvestein faction, governed. The interest of his party was to keep the house of Orange down; he courted therefore the friendship of France, and neglected that of England. The alliance between our nation and the Dutch was renewed, I think, in one thousand six hundred and sixty-two; but the latter had made a defensive league with France a little before, on the supposition principally of a war with England. The war became inevitable very soon. Cromwell had chastised them for their usurpations in trade, and the outrages and cruelties they had committed; but he had not cured them. The same spirit continued in the Dutch, the same resentments in the English: and the pique of merchants became the pique of nations. France entered into the war on the side of Holland; but the little assistance she gave the Dutch shewed plainly enough that her intention was to make these two powers waste their strength against one another, whilst she extended her conquests in the Spanish Low Countries. Her invasion of these provinces obliged De Wit to change his conduct. Hitherto he had been attached to France in the closest manner, had led his republic to serve all the purposes of France, and had renewed with the marshal D'Estrades a project of dividing the Spanish Netherlands between France and Holland, that had been taken up formerly, when Richelieu made use of it to flatter their ambition, and to engage them to prolong the war against Spain. A project not unlike to that which was held out to them by the famous preliminaries, and the extravagant barrier-treaty, in one thousand seven hundred and nine; and which engaged them to continue a war on the principle of ambition, into which they had entered with more reasonable and more moderate views.

As the private interest of the two De Wits hindered that common-wealth from being on her guard, as early as she ought to have been, against France; so the mistaken policy of the court of England, and the short views, and the profuse temper of the prince who governed, gave great advantages to Lewis the fourteenth in the pursuit of his designs. He bought Dunkirk: and your lordship knows how great a clamour was raised on that occasion against your noble ancestor; as if he alone had been answerable for the measure, and his interest had been concerned in it. I have heard our late friend Mr. George Clark, quote a witness, who was quite unexceptionable, but I cannot recall his name at present, who, many years after all these transactions, and the death of my lord Clarendon, affirmed, that the earl of Sandwich had owned to him, that he himself gave his opinion, among many others, officers, and ministers, for selling Dunkirk. Their reasons could not be good, I presume to say; but several, that might be plausible at that time, are easily guessed. A prince like king Charles, who would have made as many bad bargains as any young spendthrift, for money, finding himself thus backed, we may assure ourselves, was peremptorily determined to sell; and whatever your great grandfather's opinion was, this I am able to pronounce upon my own experience, that his treaty for the sale is no proof he was of opinion to sell. When the resolution of selling was once taken, to whom could the sale be made? To the Dutch? No. This measure would have been at least as impolitic, and, in that moment, perhaps more odious than the other. To the Spaniards? They were unable to buy: and, as low as their power was sunk, the principle of opposing it still prevailed. I have sometimes thought that the Spaniards, who were forced to make peace with Portugal, and to renounce all claim to that crown, four or five years afterwards, might have been induced to take this resolution then, if the regaining Dunkirk without any expence had been a condition proposed to them; and that the Portuguese, who, notwithstanding their alliance with England and the indirect succours that France afforded them, were little able, after the treaty especially, to support a war against Spain, might have been induced to pay the price of Dunkirk, for so great an advantage as immediate peace with Spain, and the extinction of all foreign pretences on their crown. But this speculation concerning events so long ago passed is not much to the purpose here. I proceed therefore to observe, that notwithstanding the sale of Dunkirk, and the secret leanings of our court to that of France, yet England was first to take the alarm, when Lewis the fourteenth invaded the Spanish Netherlands in one thousand six hundred and sixty-seven: and the triple alliance was the work of an English minister. It was time to take this alarm; for from the moment that the king of France claimed a right to the county of Burgundy, the dutchy of Brabant, and other portions of the Low Countries as devolved on his queen by the death of her father Philip the fourth, he pulled off the mask entirely. Volumes were written to establish, and to refute the supposed right. Your lordship no doubt will look into a controversy that has employed so many pens and so many swords; and I believe you will think it was sufficiently bold in the French to argue from customs, that regulated the course of private successions in certain provinces to a right of succeeding to the sovereignty of those provinces; and to assert the divisibility of the Spanish monarchy, with the same breath with which they asserted the indivisibility of their own; although the proofs in one case were just as good as the proofs in the other, and the fundamental law of indivisibility was at least as good a law in Spain, as either this or the Salique law was in France. But however proper it might be for the French and Austrian pens to enter into long discussions, and to appeal, on this great occasion, to the rest of Europe; the rest of Europe had a short objection to make to the plea of France, which no sophisms, no quirks of law, could evade. Spain accepted the renunciations as a real security: France gave them as such to Spain, and in effect to the rest of Europe. If they had not been thus given, and thus taken, the Spaniards would not have married their Infanta to the king of France,

whatever distress they might have endured by the pro-
longation of the war. These renunciations were renunciations of all rights whatsoever to the whole Spanish monarchy, and to every part of it. The provinces claimed by
France at this time were parts of it. To claim them, was
therefore to claim the whole; for if the renunciations were
no bar to the rights accruing to Mary Theresa on the
death of her father Philip the fourth, neither could they be
any to the rights that would accrue to her, and her children,
on the death of her brother Charles the second: an un-
healthful youth, and who at this instant was in immediate
danger of dying; for to all the complicated distempers he
brought into the world with him, the small-pox was
added. Your lordship sees how the fatal contingency of
uniting the two monarchies of France and Spain stared
mankind in the face; and yet nothing, that I can remember,
was done to prevent it: not so much as a guarantee given, or
a declaration made to assert the validity of these renunciations, and for securing the effect of them. The triple
alliance indeed stopped the progress of the French arms,
and produced the treaty of Aix la Chapelle. But England,
Sweden, and Holland, the contracting powers in this
alliance, seemed to look, and probably did look no farther.
France kept a great and important part of what she had
surprized or ravished, or purchased; for we cannot say
with any propriety that she conquered: and the Spaniards
were obliged to set all they saved to the account of gain.
The German branch of Austria had been reduced very low
in power and in credit under Ferdinand the third, by the
treaties of Westphalia, as I have said already. Lewis the
fourteenth maintained, during many years, the influence
these treaties had given him among the princes and states of

the empire. The famous capitulation made at Franckfort on the election of Leopold, who succeeded Ferdinand about the year one thousand six hundred and fifty-seven, was encouraged by the intrigues of France: and the power of France was looked upon as the sole power that could ratify and secure effectually the observation of the conditions then made. The league of the Rhine was not renewed I believe after the year one thousand six hundred and sixty-six; but though this league was not renewed, yet some of these princes and states continued in their old engagement with France: whilst others took new engagements on particular occasions, according as private and sometimes very paltry interests, and the emissaries of France in all their little courts, disposed them. In short the princes of Germany shewed no alarm at the growing ambition and power of Lewis the fourteenth, but contributed to encourage one, and to confirm the other. In such a state of things the German branch was little able to assist the Spanish branch against France, either in the war that ended by the Pyrenean treaty, or in that we are speaking of here, the short war that began in one thousand six hundred and sixty-seven, and was ended by the treaty of Aix la Chapelle, in one thousand six hundred and sixty-eight. But it was not this alone that disabled the emperor from acting with vigour in the cause of his family then, nor that has rendered the house of Austria a dead weight upon all her allies ever since. Bigotry, and its inseparable companion, cruelty, as well as the tyranny and avarice of the court of Vienna, created in those days, and has maintained in ours, almost a perpetual diversion of the imperial arms from all effectual opposition to France. I mean to speak of the troubles in Hungary. Whatever they became in their progress, they were caused

originally by the usurpations and persecutions of the
emperor, and when the Hungarians were called rebels first,
they were called so for no other reason than this, that they
would not be slaves. The dominion of the emperor being
less supportable than that of the Turks, this unhappy
people opened a door to the latter to infest the empire,
instead of making their country what it had been before,
a barrier against the Ottoman power. France became a
sure, though secret ally of the Turks, as well as the
Hungarians, and has found her account in it, by keeping the
emperor in perpetual alarms on that side, while she has
ravaged the empire and the Low Countries on the other.
Thus we saw, thirty-two years ago, the arms of France and
Bavaria in possession of Passau, and the malcontents of
Hungary in the suburbs of Vienna. In a word, when
Lewis the fourteenth made the first essay of his power, by
the war of one thousand six hundred and sixty-seven, and
founded, as it were, the councils of Europe concerning his
pretensions on the Spanish succession, he found his power
to be great beyond what his neighbours or even he perhaps
thought it: great by the wealth, and greater by the united
spirit of his people; greater still by the ill policy, and divided
interests that governed those who had a superior common
interest to oppose him. He found that the members of the
triple alliance did not see, or seeing did not think proper to
own that they saw, the injustice, and the consequence of his
pretensions. They contented themselves to give to Spain an
act of guaranty for securing the execution of the treaty of
Aix la Chapelle. He knew even then how ill the guarantee
would be observed by two of them at least, by England and
by Sweden. The treaty itself was nothing more than a composition between the bully and the bullied. Tournay, and

Lisle, and Doway, and other places that I have forgot, were yielded to him: and he restored the county of Burgundy, according to the option that Spain made, against the interest and expectation too of the Dutch, when an option was forced upon her. The king of Spain compounded for his possession: but the emperor compounded at the same time for his succession, by a private eventual treaty of partition, which the commander of Gremonville and the count of Aversberg signed at Vienna. The same Leopold, who exclaimed so loudly in one thousand six hundred and ninety-eight, against any partition of the Spanish monarchy, and refused to submit to that which England and Holland had then made, made one himself in one thousand six hundred and sixty-eight, with so little regard to these two powers, that the whole ten provinces were thrown into the lot of France.

There is no room to wonder if such experience as Lewis the fourteenth had upon this occasion, and such a face of affairs in Europe, raising his hopes, raised his ambition: and if, in making peace at Aix la Chapelle, he meditated a new war, the war of one thousand six hundred and seventy-two; the preparations he made for it, by negociations in all parts, by alliances whereever he found ingression, and by the increase of his forces, were equally proofs of ability, industry, and power. I shall not descend into these particulars: your lordship will find them pretty well detailed in the memorials of that time. But one of the alliances he made I must mention, though I mention it with the utmost regret and indignation. England was fatally engaged to act a part in this conspiracy against the peace and the liberty of Europe, nay, against her own peace and her own liberty; for a bubble's part it was, equally wicked and impolitic. Forgive the terms I use, my lord: none can be too strong. The principles of the triple alliance just and wise, and worthy of a king of England, were laid aside. Then, the progress of the French arms was to be checked, the ten provinces were to be saved, and by saving them, the barrier of Holland was to be preserved. Now, we joined our councils and our arms to those of France, in a project that could not be carried on at all, as it was easy to foresee, and as the event shewed, unless it was carried on against Spain, the emperor, and most of the princes of Germany, as well as the Dutch; and which could not be carried on success-fully, without leaving the ten provinces entirely at the mercy of France and giving her pretence and opportunity of ravaging the empire, and extending her conquests on the Rhine. The medal of Van Beuninghen, and other pretences that France took for attacking the states of the Low Countries, were ridiculous. They imposed on no one: and the true object of Lewis the fourteenth was manifest to all. But what could a king of England mean? Charles the second had reasons of resentment against the Dutch, and just ones too no doubt. Among the rest, it was not easy for him to forget the affront he had suffered, and the loss he had sustained, when, depending on the peace that was ready to be signed, and that was signed at Breda in July, he neglected to fit out his fleet; and when that of Holland, commanded by Ruyter, with Cornelius de Wit on board as deputy or commissioner of the states, burnt his ships at Chatham in June. The famous perpetual edict, as it was called, but did not prove in the event, against the election of a state-holder, which John de Wit promoted, carried, and obliged the prince of Orange to swear to maintain a very few days after the conclusion of the peace at Breda, might be another motive in the breast of king Charles the second: as it was certainly a pretence of revenge on the Dutch, or at least on the De Wits and the Louvestein faction, that ruled almost despotically in that commonwealth. But it is plain that neither these reasons, nor others of a more ancient date, determined him to this alliance with France; since he contracted the triple alliance within four or five months after the two events, I have mentioned, happened. What then did he mean? Did he mean to acquire one of the seven provinces, and divide them, as the Dutch had twice treated for the division of the ten, with France? I believe not; but this I believe, that his inclinations were favourable to the popish interest in general, and that he meant to make himself more absolute at home; that he thought it necessary to this end to humble the Dutch, to reduce their power, and perhaps to change the form of their government; to deprive his subjects of the correspondence with a neighbouring protestant and free state, and of all hope of succour and support from thence in their opposition to him; in a word, to abet the designs of France on the continent, that France might abet his designs on his own kingdom. This, I say, I believe; and this I should venture to affirm, if I had in my hands to produce, and was at liberty to quote, the private relations I have read formerly, drawn up by those who were no enemies to such designs, and on the authority of those who were parties to them. But whatever king Charles the second meant, certain it is that his conduct established the superiority of France in Europe.

But this charge, however, must not be confined to him alone. Those who were nearer the danger, those who were exposed to the immediate attacks of France, and even those who were her rivals for the same succession, have either assisted her, or engaged to remain neuters; a strange fatality prevailed, and produced such a conjuncture as can hardly be paralleled in history. Your lordship will observe with astonishment even in the beginning of the year one thousand six hundred and seventy-two, all the neighbours of France acting as if they had nothing to fear from her, and some as if they had much to hope, by helping her to oppress the Dutch and sharing with her the spoils of that commonwealth. "Delenda est Carthago," was the cry in England, and seemed too a maxim on the continent.

In the course of the same year, you will observe that all these powers took the alarm, and began to unite in opposition to France. Even England thought it time to interpose in favour of the Dutch. The consequences of this alarm, of this sudden turn in the policy of Europe and of that which happened by the massacre of the De Wits, and the elevation of the prince of Orange, in the government of the seven provinces, saved these provinces, and stopped the rapid progress of the arms of France. Lewis the fourteenth indeed surprised the seven provinces in this war, as he had surprised the ten in that of one thousand six hundred and sixty-seven, and ravaged defenceless countries with armies sufficient to conquer them, if they had been prepared to resist. In the war of one thousand six hundred and seventy-two, he had little less than one hundred and fifty thousand men on foot, besides the bodies, of English, Swiss, Italians, and Swedes, that amounted to thirty or forty thousand more. With this mighty force, he took forty places in forty days, imposed extravagant conditions of peace, played the monarch a little while at Utrecht; and as soon as the Dutch recovered from their consternation, and, animated by the example of the prince of Orange and the hopes of succour, refused these conditions, he went back to Versailles, and left his generals to carry on his enterprize: which they did with so little success, that Grave and Mae-stricht alone remained to him of all the boasted conquests he had made; and even these he offered two years afterwards to restore, if by that concession he could have prevailed on the Dutch at that time to make peace with him. But they were not yet disposed to abandon their allies; for allies now they had. The emperor and the king of Spain had engaged in the quarrel against France, and many of the princes of the empire had done the same. Not all. The Bavarian continued obstinate in his neutrality, and to mention no more, the Swedes made a great diversion in favour of France in the empire; where the duke of Hanover abetted their designs as much as he could, for he was a zealous partisan of France, though the other princes of his house acted for the common cause. I descend into no more particulars. The war that Lewis the fourteenth kindled by attacking in so violent a manner the Dutch commonwealth, and by making so arbitrary an use of his first success, became general, in the Low Countries, in Spain, in Sicily, on the upper and lower Rhine, in Denmark, in Sweden, and in the provinces of Germany belonging to these two crowns; on the Medi-terranean, the Ocean, and the Baltic. France supported this war with advantage on every side: and when your lordship considers in what manner it was carried on against her, you will not be surprised that she did so. Spain had spirit, but too little strength to maintain her power in Sicily, where Messina had revolted; to defend her frontier on that side of the Pyrenees; and to resist the great efforts of the French in the Low Countries. The empire was divided; and, even among the princes who acted against France, there was neither union in their councils, nor concert in their projects, nor order in preparations, nor vigour in execution: and, to say the truth, there was not, in the whole confederacy, a man whose abilities could make him a match for the prince of Conde or the marshal of Turenne; nor many who were in any degree equal to Luxemburg, Crequi, Schomberg, and other generals of inferior note, who commanded the armies of France. The emperor took this very time to make new invasions on the liberties of Hungary, and to oppress his protestant subjects. The prince of Orange alone acted with invincible firmness, like a patriot, and a hero. Neither the seductions of France nor those of England, neither the temptations of ambition nor those of private interest could make him swerve from the true interest of his country, nor from the common interest of Europe. He had raised more sieges, and lost more battles, it was said, than any general of his age had done. Be it so. But his defeats were manifestly due in a great measure to circumstances independent on him: and that spirit, which even these defeats could not depress, was all his own. He had difficulties in his own commonwealth; the governors of the Spanish Low Countries crossed his measures sometimes: the German allies disappointed and broke them often: and it is not improbable that he was frequently betrayed. He was so perhaps even by Souches, the imperial general: a Frenchman according to Bayle, and a pensioner of Louvois according to common report, and very strong appearances. He had not yet credit and authority sufficient to make him a centre of union to a whole confederacy, the soul that animated and directed so great a body. He came to be such afterwards; but at the time spoken of he could not take so great a part upon him. No other prince or general was equal to it; and the consequences of this defect appeared almost in every operation. France was surrounded by a multitude of enemies, all intent to demolish her power. But, like the builders of Babel, they spoke different languages; and as those could not build, these could not demolish, for want of understanding one another. France improved this advantage by her arms, and more by her negociations. Nimeghen was, after Cologn, the scene of these. England was the mediating power, and I know not whether our Charles the second did not serve her purposes more usefully in the latter, and under the character of mediator, than he did or could have done by joining his arms to her's, and acting as her ally. The Dutch were induced to sign a treaty with him, that broke the confederacy, and gave great advantage to France: for the purport of it was to oblige France and Spain to make peace on a plan to be proposed to them, and no mention was made in it of the other allies that I remember. The Dutch were glad to get out of an expensive war. France promised to restore Maestricht to them, and Maestricht was the only place that remained unrecovered of all they had lost. They dropped Spain at Nimeghen, as they had dropped France at Munster, but many circumstances concurred to give a much worse grace to their abandoning of Spain, than to their abandoning of France. I need not specify them. This only I would observe: when they made a separate peace at Munster, they left an ally who was in condition to carry on the war alone with advantage, and they presumed to impose no terms upon him: when they made a separate peace at Nimeghen, they abandoned an ally who was in no condition to carry on the war alone, and who was reduced to accept whatever terms the common enemy prescribed. In their great distress in

one thousand six hundred and seventy-three, they engaged
to restore Maestricht to the Spaniards as soon as it should
be retaken: it was not retaken, and they accepted it for
themselves as the price of the separate peace they made with
France. The Dutch had engaged farther, to make neither
peace nor truce with the king of France, till that prince
consented to restore to Spain all he had conquered since the
Pyrenean treaty. But, far from keeping this promise in any
tolerable degree, Lewis the fourteenth acquired, by the
plan imposed on Spain at Nimeghen, besides the county of
Burgundy, so many other countries and towns on the side
of the ten Spanish provinces, that these, added to the places
he kept of those which had been yielded to him by the
treaty of Aix la Chapelle (for some of little consequence he
restored), put into his hands the principal strength of that
barrier, against which we goaded ourselves almost to death
in the last great war; and made good the saying of the
marshal of Schomberg, that to attack this barrier was to take
the beast by his horns. I know very well what may be said
to excuse the Dutch. The emperor was more intent to
tyrannize his subjects on one side, than to defend them on
the other. He attempted little against France, and the little
he did attempt was ill ordered, and worse executed. The
assistance of the princes of Germany was often uncertain,
and always expensive. Spain was already indebted to
Holland for great sums; greater still must be advanced to
her if the war continued: and experience shewed that France
was able, and would continue, to prevail against her present
enemies. The triple league had stopped her progress, and
obliged her to abandon the county of Burgundy; but
Sweden was now engaged in the war on the side of France,
as England had been in the beginning of it: and England

was now privately favourable to her interests, as Sweden had been in the beginning of it. The whole ten provinces would have been subdued in the course of a few campaigns more: and it was better for Spain and the Dutch too, that part should be saved by accepting a sort of composition, than the whole be risqued by refusing it. This might be alledged to excuse the conduct of the States General, in imposing hard terms on Spain; in making none for their other allies, and in signing alone: by which steps they gave France an opportunity that she improved with great dexterity of management, the opportunity of treating with the confederates one by one, and of beating them by detail in the cabinet, if I may so say, as she had often done in the field. I shall not compare these reasons, which were but too well founded in fact, and must appear plausible at least, with other considerations that might be, and were at the time, insisted upon. I confine myself to a few observations, which every knowing and impartial man must admit. Your lordship will observe, first, that the fatal principle of compounding with Lewis the fourteenth, from the time that his pretensions, his power, and the use he made of it, began to threaten Europe, prevailed still more at Nimeghen than it had prevailed at Aix: so that although he did not obtain to the full, all he attempted, yet the dominions of France were by common consent, on every treaty, more and more extended; her barriers on all sides were more and more strengthened; those of her neighbours were more and more weakened; and that power, which was to assert one day, against the rest of Europe, the pretended rights of the house of Bourbon to the Spanish monarchy was more and more established, and rendered truly formidable in such hands at least, during the course of the first eighteen years of the period. Your lordship will please to observe in the second place, that the extreme weakness of one branch of Austria, and the miserable conduct of both; the poverty of some of the princes of the empire, and the disunion, and, to speak plainly, the mercenary policy of all of them; in short, the confined views, the false notions, and, to speak as plainly of my own as of other nations, the iniquity of the councils of England, not only hindered the growth of this power from being stopped in time, but nursed it up into strength almost insuperable by any future confederacy. A third observation is this: If the excuses made for the conduct of the Dutch at Nimeghen are not sufficient, they too must come in for their share in this condemnation, even after the death of the De Wits; as they were to be condemned most justly, during that administration, for abetting and favouring France. If these excuses, grounded on their inability to pursue any longer a war, the principal profit of which was to accrue to their confederates, for that was the case after the year one thousand six hundred and seventy-three, or one thousand six hundred and seventy-four, and the principal burden of which was thrown on them by their confederates; if these are sufficient, they should not have acted for decency's sake as well as out of good policy, the part they did act in one thousand seven hundred and eleven, and one thousand seven hundred and twelve, towards the late queen, who had complaints of the same kind, in a much higher degree, and with circumstances much more aggravating, to make of them, of the emperor, and of all the princes of Germany; and who was far from treating them and their other allies, at that time as they treated Spain and their other allies in one thousand six hundred and seventy-eight. Immediately after the Dutch had made their peace,

that of Spain was signed with France. The emperor's
treaty with this crown and that of Sweden was concluded in
the following year: and Lewis the fourteenth being now at
liberty to assist his ally, whilst he had tied up the powers
with whom he had treated from assisting theirs, he soon
forced the king of Denmark and the elector of Brandenburg
to restore all they had taken from the Swedes, and to conclude the peace of the north. In all these treaties he gave the
law, and he was now at the highest point of his grandeur.
He continued at this point for several years, and in this
heighth of his power he prepared those alliances against it,
under the weight of which he was at last well-nigh oppressed; and might have been reduced as low as the general
interest of Europe required, if some of the causes, which
worked now, had not continued to work in his favour, and
if his enemies had not proved, in their turn of fortune, as
insatiable as prosperity had rendered him.

After he had made peace with all the powers with whom
he had been in war, he continued to vex both Spain and the
empire, and to extend his conquests in the Low Countries,
and on the Rhine, both by the pen and the sword. He
erected the chambers of Metz and of Brisach, where his own
subjects were prosecutors, witnesses, and judges all at once.
Upon the decisions of these tribunals, he seized into his
own hands, under the notion of dependencies and the
pretence of re-unions, whatever towns or districts of
country tempted his ambition, or suited his conveniency:
and added, by these and by other means, in the midst of
peace, more territories to those the late treaties had yielded
to him, than he could have got by continuing the war. He
acted afterwards, in the support of all this, without any
bounds or limits. His glory was a reason for attacking

Holland in one thousand six hundred and seventy-two, and his conveniency a reason for many of the attacks he made on others afterwards. He took Luxemburg by force: he stole Strasburg; he bought Cassal: and, whilst he waited the opportunity of acquiring to his family the crown of Spain, he was not without thoughts, nor hopes perhaps, of bringing into it the imperial crown likewise. Some of the cruelties he exercised in the empire may be ascribed to his disappointment in this view: I say some of them, because in the war ended by the treaty of Nimeghen, he had already exercised many. Though the French writers endeavour to slide over them, to palliate them, and to impute them particularly to the English that were in their service, for even this one of their writers has the front to advance: yet these cruelties unheard of among civilized nations, must be granted to have been ordered by the counsels, and executed by the arms of France, in the Palatinate, and in other parts.

If Lewis the fourteenth could have contented himself with the acquisitions that were confirmed to him by the treaties of one thousand six hundred and seventy-eight, and one thousand six hundred and seventy-nine, and with the authority and reputation which he then gained; it is plain that he would have prevented the alliances that were afterwards formed against him; and that he might have regained his credit amongst the princes of the empire, where he had one family-alliance by the marriage of his brother to the daughter of the elector Palatine, and another by that of his son to the sister of the elector of Bavaria; where Sweden was closely attached to him, and where the same principles of private interest would have soon attached others as closely. He might have remained not only the principal, but the directing power of Europe, and have held this rank with all the glory imaginable, till the death of the king of Spain, or some other object of great ambition, had determined him to act another part. But, instead of this, he continued to vex and provoke all those who were, unhappily for them, his neighbours, and that, in many instances for trifles. An example of this kind occurs to me. On the death of the duke of Deux Ponts, he seized that little inconsiderable dutchy, without any regard to the indisputable right of the king of Sweden, to the services that crown had rendered him, or to the want he might have of that alliance hereafter. The consequence was, that Sweden entered, with the emperor, the king of Spain, the elector of Bavaria, and the States General, into the alliance of guaranty, as it was called, about the year one thousand six hundred and eighty-three, and into the famous league of Ausburg, in one thousand six hundred and eighty-six.

Since I have mentioned this league, and since we may date from it a more general and a more concerted opposition to France than there had been before; give me leave to recall some of the reflections that have presented themselves to my mind, in considering what I have read, and what I have heard related, concerning the passages of that time. They will be of use to form our judgment concerning later passages. If the king of France became an object of aversion on account of any invasions he made, any deviations from public faith, any barbarities exercised where his arms prevailed, or the persecution of his protestant subjects; the emperor deserved to be such an object, at least as much as he, on the same accounts. The emperor was so too, but with this difference relatively to the political system of the west: the Austrian ambition and bigotry exerted themselves in distant countries, whose interests were not considered as a part of this system; for, otherwise there would have been as much reason for assisting the people of Hungary and of Transylvania against the emperor, as there had been formerly for assisting the people of the seven united provinces against Spain, or as there have been lately for assisting them against France: but the ambition and bigotry of Lewis the fourteenth were exerted in the Low Countries, on the Rhine, in Italy, and in Spain, in the very midst of this system, if I may say so, and with success that could not fail to subvert it in time. The power of the house of Austria, that had been feared too long, was feared no longer: and that of the house of Bourbon, by having been feared too late, was now grown terrible. The emperor was so intent on the establishment of his absolute power in Hungary, that he exposed the empire doubly to desolation and ruin for the sake of it. He left the frontier almost quite defenceless on the side of the Rhine, against the inroads and ravages of France: and by shewing no mercy to the Hungarians, nor keeping any faith with them, he forced that miserable people into alliances with the Turk, who invaded the empire, and besieged Vienna. Even this event had no effect upon him. Your lordship will find, that Sobieski king of Poland, who had forced the Turks to raise the siege, and had fixed the imperial crown that tottered on his head, could not prevail on him to take those measures by which alone it was possible to cover the empire, to secure the King of Spain, and to reduce that power who was probably one day to dispute with him this prince's succession. Tekeli and the malecontents made such demands as none but a tyrant could refuse, the preservation of their ancient privileges, liberty of conscience, the convocation of a free diet or parliament, and others of less importance. All was in vain. The war continued with them, and with the Turks, and France was left at liberty to push her enterprizes almost without opposition, against Germany and the Low Countries. The distress in both was so great, that the States General saw no other expedient for stopping the progress of the French arms, than a cessation of hostilities, or a truce of twenty years; which they negociated, and which was accepted by the emperor and the king of Spain on the terms that Lewis the fourteenth thought fit to offer. By these terms he was to remain in full and quiet possession of all he had acquired since the years one thousand six hundred and seventy-eight, and one thousand six hundred and seventy-nine; among which acquisitions that of Luxemburg and that of Strasburg were comprehended. The conditions of this truce were so advantageous to France, that all their intrigues were employed to obtain a definitive treaty of peace upon the same conditions. But this was neither the interest nor the intention of the other contracting powers. The imperial arms had been very successful against the Turks. This success as well as the troubles that followed upon it in the Ottoman armies, and at the Porte, gave a reasonable expectation of concluding a peace on that side: and, this peace concluded, the emperor, and the empire, and the king of Spain would have been in a much better posture to treat with France. With these views, that were wise and just, the league of Ausburg was made between the emperor, the kings of Spain and Sweden, as princes of the empire, and the other circles and princes. This league was purely defensive. An express article declared it to be so: and as it had no other regard, it was not only conformable to the laws and constitutions of the empire, and to the practice of all nations, but even to the terms of the act of truce so lately concluded. This pretence therefore for breaking the truce, seizing the electorate of Cologn, invading the Palatinate, besieging Philipsburg, and carrying unexpected and undeclared war into the empire, could not be supported: nor is it possible to read the reasons published by France at this time, and drawn from her fears of the imperial power, without laughter. As little pretence was there to complain, that the emperor refused to convert at once the truce into a definitive treaty; since, if he had done so, he would have confirmed in a lump, and without any discussion, all the arbitrary decrees of those chambers, or courts, that France had erected to cover her usurpations; and would have given up almost a sixth part of the provinces of the empire, that France one way or other had possessed herself of. The pretensions of the Dutchess of Orleans on the succession of her father, and her brother, which were disputed by the then elector Palatine, and were to be determined by the laws and customs of the empire, afforded as little pretence for beginning this war, as any of the former allegations. The exclusion of the cardinal of Furstenberg, who had been elected to the archbishoprick of Cologn, was capable of being aggravated: but even in this case his most christian majesty opposed his judgment and his authority against the judgment and authority of that holy father, whose eldest son he was proud to be called. In short, the true reason why Lewis the fourteenth began that cruel war with the empire, two years after he had concluded a cessation of hostilities for twenty, was this: he resolved to keep what he had got; and therefore he resolved to encourage the Turks to continue the war. He did this effectually, by invading Germany at the very instant when the Sultan was suing for peace. Notwithstanding this, the Turks were in treaty again the following year: and good policy should have obliged the emperor, since he could not hope to carry on this war and that against France, at the same time with vigour and effect, to conclude a peace with the least dangerous enemy of the two. The decision of this dispute with France could not be deferred, his designs against the Hungarians were in part accomplished, for his son was declared king, and the settlement of that crown in his family was made; and the rest of these, as well as those that he formed against the Turks, might be deferred. But the councils of Vienna judged differently, and insisted even at this critical moment on the most exorbitant terms; on some of such a nature, that the Turks shewed more humanity and a better sense of religion in refusing, than they in asking them. Thus the war went on in Hungary, and proved a constant diversion in favour of France, during the whole course of that which Lewis the fourteenth began at this time: for the treaty of Carlowitz was posterior to that of Ryswic. The empire, Spain, England, and Holland engaged in the war with France, and on them the emperor left the burden of it. In the short war of one thousand six hundred and sixty-seven, he was not so much as a party, and instead of assisting the king of Spain, which, it must be owned, he was in no good condition of doing, he bargained for dividing that prince's succession, as I have observed above. In the war of one thousand six hundred and seventy-two he made some feeble efforts. In this of one thousand six hundred and eighty-eight he did still less; and in the war which broke out at the beginning of the present century he did nothing, at least after the first campaign in Italy, and after the engagements that England and Holland took by the grand alliance. In a word, from the time that an opposition to France became a common cause in Europe, the house of Austria has been a clog upon it in many instances, and of considerable assistance to it in none. The accession of England to this cause, which was brought about by the revolution of one thousand six hundred and eighty-eight, might have made amends, and more than amends, one would think, for this defect, and have thrown superiority of power and of success on the side of the confederates, with whom she took part against France. This, I say, might be imagined, without over-rating the power of England, or undervaluing that of France; and it was imagined at that time. How it proved otherwise in the event; how France came triumphant out of the war that ended by the treaty of Ryswic, and though she gave up a great deal, yet preserved the greatest and the best part of her conquest and acquisitions made since the treaties of Westphalia, and the Pyrenées; how she acquired, by the gift of Spain, that whole monarchy for one of her princes, though she had no reason to expect the least part of it without a war at one time, nor the great lot of it even by a war at any time; in short, how she wound up advantageously the ambitious system she had been fifty years in weaving; how she concluded a war, in which she was defeated on every side, and wholly exhausted, with little diminution of the provinces and barriers acquired to France, and with the quiet possession of Spain and the Indies to a prince of the house of Bourbon: all this, my lord, will be the subject of your researches, when you come down to the latter part of the last period of modern history.

The same subject continued from the year one thousand six hundred and eighty-eight.

Your lordship will find that the objects proposed by the alliance of one thousand six hundred and eighty-nine between the emperor and the States, to which England acceded, and which was the foundation of the whole confederacy then formed, were no less than to restore all things to the terms of the Westphalian and Pyrenean treaties, by the war; and to preserve them in that state, after the war, by a defensive alliance and guaranty of the same confederate powers against France. The particular as well as general meaning of this engagement was plain enough: and if it had not been so, the sense of it would have been sufficiently determined, by that separate article, in which England and Holland obliged themselves to assist the "house of Austria, in taking and keeping possession of the Spanish monarchy, whenever the case should happen of the death of Charles the second, without lawful heirs." This engagement was double, and thereby relative to the whole political system of Europe, alike affected by the power and pretensions of France. Hitherto the power of France had been alone regarded, and her pretensions seemed to have been forgot: or to what purpose should they have been remembered, whilst Europe was so unhappily constituted, that the states, at whose expence she encreased her power, and their friends and allies, thought that they did enough upon every occasion if they made some tolerable composition with her? They who were not in circumstances to refuse confirming present, were little likely to take effectual measures against future usurpations. But now, as the alarm was greater than ever, by the outrages that France had committed, and the intrigues she had carried on; by the little regard she had shewn to public faith, and by the airs of authority she had assumed twenty years together: so was the spirit against her raised to an higher pitch, and the means of reducing her power, or at least of checking it, were increased. The princes and states who had neglected or favoured the growth of this power, which all of them had done in their turns, saw their error; saw the necessity of repairing it, and saw that unless they could check the power of France by uniting a power superior to her's, it would be impossible to hinder her from succeeding in her great designs on the Spanish succession. The court of England had submitted, not many years before, to abet her usurpations, and the king of England had stooped to be her pensioner. But the crime was not national. On the contrary, the nation had cried out loudly against it, even whilst it was committing: and as soon as ever the abdication of King James, and the elevation of the prince of Orange to the throne of England happened, the nation engaged with all imaginable zeal in the common cause of Europe, to reduce the exorbitant power of France, to prevent her future and to revenge her past attempts; for even a spirit of revenge prevailed, and the war was a war of anger as well as of interest.

Unhappily this zeal was neither well conducted, nor well seconded. It was zeal without success in the first of the two wars that followed the year one thousand six hundred and eighty-eight; and zeal without knowledge, in both of them. I enter into no detail concerning the events of these two

wars. This only I observe on the first of them, that the
treaties of Ryswic were far from answering the ends proposed and the engagements taken by the first grand alliance.
The power of France, with respect to extent of dominions
and strength of barrier, was not reduced to the terms of the
Pyrenean treaty, no not to those of the treaty of Nimeghen.
Lorrain was restored indeed with very considerable re-
serves, and the places taken or usurped on the other side of
the Rhine: but then Strasburg was yielded up absolutely to
France by the emperor, and by the empire. The concessions
to Spain were great, but so were the conquests and the
encroachments made upon her by France, since the treaty of
Nimeghen: and she got little at Ryswic, I believe nothing
more than she had saved at Nimeghen before. All these
concessions, however, as well as the acknowledgement of
King William, and others made by Lewis the fourteenth
after he had taken Ath and Barcelona, even during the
course of the negociations, compared with the losses and
repeated defeats of the allies and the ill state of the confederacy, surprised the generality of mankind, who had not been
accustomed to so much moderation and generosity on the
part of this prince. But the pretensions of the house of
Bourbon on the Spanish succession remained the same.
Nothing had been done to weaken them; nothing was
prepared to oppose them: and the opening of this succession
was visibly at hand: for Charles the second had been in
immediate danger of dying about this time. His death could
not be a remote event: and all the good queen's endeavours
to be got with child had proved ineffectual. The league
dissolved, all the forces of the confederates dispersed, and
many disbanded; France continuing armed, her forces by
sea and land encreased and held in readiness to act on all

sides, it was plain that the confederates had failed in the first object of the grand alliance, that of reducing the power of France; by succeeding in which alone they could have been able to keep the second engagement, that of securing the succession of Spain to the house of Austria.

After this peace, what remained to be done? In the whole nature of things there remained but three. To abandon all care of the Spanish succession was one; to compound with France upon this succession was another; and to prepare, like her, during the interval of peace, to make an advantageous war whenever Charles the second should die, was a third. Now the first of these was to leave Spain, and in leaving Spain, to leave all Europe in some sort at the mercy of France; since whatever disposition the Spaniards should make of their crown, they were quite unable to support it against France; since the emperor could do little without his alliance; and since Bavaria, the third pretender, could do still less, and might find, in such a case, his account perhaps better in treating with the house of Bourbon than with that of Austria. More needs not be said on this head; but on the other two, which I shall consider together, several facts are proper to be mentioned, and several reflections necessary to be made.

We might have counter-worked, no doubt, in their own methods of policy, the councils of France, who made peace to dissolve the confederacy, and great concessions, with very suspicious generosity, to gain the Spaniards: we might have waited, like them, that is in arms, the death of Charles the second, and have fortified in the mean time the dispositions of the king, the court, and people of Spain, against the pretensions of France: we might have made the peace which was made some time after that, between the emperor and the Turks, and have obliged the former at any rate to have secured the peace of Hungary, and to have prepared by these and other expedients, for the war that would inevitably break out on the death of the king of Spain.

But all such measures were rendered impracticable, by the emperor chiefly. Experience had shewn, that the powers who engaged in alliance with him must expect to take the whole burden of his cause upon themselves; and that Hungary would maintain a perpetual diversion in favour of France, since he could not resolve to lighten the tyrannical yoke he had established in that country and in Transylvania, nor his ministers to part with the immense confiscations they had appropriated to themselves. Past experience shewed this: and the experience that followed, confirmed it very fatally. But further; there was not only little assistance to be expected from him by those who should engage in his quarrel: he did them hurt of another kind, and deprived them of many advantages by false measures of policy and unskilful negociations. Whilst the death of Charles the second was expected almost daily, the court of Vienna seemed to have forgot the court of Madrid, and all the pretensions on that crown. When the count d'Harrach was sent thither, the imperial councils did something worse. The king of Spain was ready to declare the arch-duke Charles his successor; he was desirous to have this young prince sent into Spain: the bent of the people was in favour of Austria, or it had been so, and might have been easily turned the same way again: at court no cabal was yet formed in favour of Bourbon, and a very weak intrigue was on foot in favour of the electoral prince of Bavaria. Not only Charles might have been on the spot ready to reap the succession, but a German army might have been there to

defend it; for the court of Madrid insisted on having twelve
thousand of these troops, and, rather than not to have them
offered to contribute to the payment of them privately:
because it would have been too unpopular among the
Spaniards, and too prejudicial to the Austrian interest, to
have had it known that the emperor declined the payment of
a body of his own troops that were demanded to secure that
monarchy to his son. These proposals were half refused,
and half evaded: and in return to the offer of the crown of
Spain to the archduke, the imperial councils asked the
government of Milan for him. They thought it a point of
deep policy to secure the Italian provinces, and to leave to
England and Holland the care of the Low Countries, of
Spain, and the Indies. By declining these proposals, the
house of Austria renounced in some sort the whole succession: at least she gave England and Holland reasons, whatever engagements these powers had taken, to refuse the
harder task of putting her into possession by force; when
she might, and would not, procure to the English and Dutch,
and her other allies, the easier task of defending her in this
possession.

I said that the measures mentioned above were rendered
impracticable, by the emperor chiefly, because they were
rendered so likewise by other circumstances at the same
conjuncture. A principal one I shall mention, and it shall
be drawn from the state of our own country, and the disposition of our people. Let us take this up from king
William's accession to our crown. During the whole
progress that Lewis the fourteenth made towards such
exorbitant power, as gave him well-grounded hopes of
acquiring at last to his family the Spanish monarchy,
England had been either an idle spectator of all that passed

on the continent, or a faint and uncertain ally against France, or a warm and sure ally on her side, or a partial mediator between her and the powers confederated in their common defence. The revolution produced as great a change in our foreign conduct as in our domestic establishment: and our nation engaged with great spirit in the war of one thousand six hundred and eighty-eight. But then this spirit was rash, presumptuous and ignorant, ill conducted at home, and ill seconded abroad: all which has been touched already. We had waged no long war on the continent, nor been very deeply concerned in foreign confederacies, since the fourteenth and fifteenth centuries. The history of Edward the third, however, and of the first twelve or fifteen years of Henry the sixth might have taught us some general but useful lessons, drawn from remote times, but applicable to the present. So might the example of Henry the eighth, who squandered away great sums for the profit of taking a town, or the honour of having an emperor in his pay; and who divided afterwards by treaty the kingdom of France between himself and Charles the fifth, with success so little answerable to such an undertaking, that it is hard to believe his imperial and English majesty were both in earnest. If they were so, they were both the bubbles of their presumption. But it seems more likely that Henry the eighth was bubbled on this occasion by the great hopes that Charles held out to flatter his vanity: as he had been bubbled by his father-in-law, Ferdinand, at the beginning of his reign, in the war of Navarre. But these reflections were not made, nor had we enough considered the example of Elizabeth, the last of our princes who had made any considerable figure abroad, and from whom we might have learned to act with vigour, but to engage with caution, and always to proportion our assistance according to our abilities, and the real necessities of our allies. The frontiers of France were now so fortified, her commerce and her naval force were so encreased, her armies were grown so numerous, her troops were so disciplined, so inured to war, and so animated by a long course of successful campaigns, that they who looked on the situation of Europe could not fail to see how difficult the enterprize of reducing her power was become. Difficult as it was, we were obliged on every account, and by reasons of all kinds, to engage in it: but then we should have engaged with more forecast, and have conducted ourselves in the management of it, not with less alacrity and spirit, but with more order, more œconomy, and a better application of our efforts. But they who governed were glad to engage us at any rate: and we entered on this great scheme of action, as our nation is too apt to do, hurried on by the ruling passion of the day. I have been told by several, who were on the stage of the world at this time, that the generality of our people believed, and were encouraged to believe, the war could not be long, if the king was vigorously supported: and there in a humdrum speech of a speaker, of the house of commons, I think, who humbly desired his majesty to take this opportunity of reconquering his ancient dutchy of Acquitain. We were soon awakened from these gaudy dreams. In seven or eight years no impression had been made on France that was besieged as it were on every side: and after repeated defeats in the Low Countries, where king William laid the principal stress of the war, his sole triumph was the retaking of Namur, that had been taken by the French a few years before. Unsustained by success abroad, we are not to wonder that the spirit flagged at home; nor that the dis-

contents of those who were averse to the established government uniting with the far greater number of those who
disliked the administration, inflamed the general discontents
of the nation, oppressed with taxes, pillaged by usurers,
plundered at sea, and disappointed at land. As we run into
extremes always, some would have continued this war at
any rate, even at the same rate: but it was not possible they
should prevail in such a situation of affairs, and such a disposition of minds. They who got by the war, and made
immense fortunes by the necessities of the public, were not
so numerous nor so powerful as they have been since. The
moneyed interest was not yet a rival able to cope with the
landed interest, either in the nation or in parliament. The
great corporations that had been erected more to serve the
turn of party, than for any real national use, aimed indeed
even then at the strength and influence which they have
since acquired in the legislature; but they had not made the
same progress by promoting national corruption, as they
and the court have made since. In short, the other extreme
prevailed. The generality of people grew as fond of getting
out of the war, as they had been of entering into it: and
thus far perhaps, considering how it had been conducted,
they were not much to be blamed. But this was not all;
for when king William had made the peace, our martial
spirit became at once so pacific, that we seemed resolved to
meddle no more in the affairs of the continent, at least to
employ our arms no more in the quarrels that might arise
there: and accordingly we reduced our troops in England to
seven thousand men.

I have sometimes considered, in reflecting on these
passages, what I should have done, if I had sat in parliament
at that time: and have been forced to own myself, that I

should have voted for disbanding the army then; as I voted in the following parliament for censuring the partition-treaties. I am forced to own this, because I remember how imperfect my notions were of the situation of Europe in that extraordinary crisis, and how much I saw the true interest of my own country in an half light. But, my lord, I own it with some shame; because in truth nothing could be more absurd than the conduct we held. What! because we had not reduced the power of France by the war, nor excluded the house of Bourbon from the Spanish succession, nor compounded with her upon it by the peace; and because the house of Austria had not helped herself, nor put it into our power to help her with more advantage and better prospect of success—were we to leave that whole succession open to the invasions of France, and to suffer even the contingency to subsist, of seeing those monarchies united? What! because it was become extravagant, after the trials so lately made, to think ourselves any longer engaged by treaty or obliged by good policy, to put the house of Austria in possession of the whole Spanish monarchy, and to defend her in this possession by force of arms, were we to leave the whole at the mercy of France? If we were not to do so, if we were not to do one of the three things that I said above remained to be done, and if the emperor put it out of our power to do another of them with advantage; were we to put it still more out of our power, and to wait unarmed for the death of the king of Spain? In fine, if we had not the prospect of disputing with France, so success-fully as we might have had it, the Spanish succession, when-ever it should be open; were we not only to shew by disarming, that we would not dispute it at all, but to censure likewise the second of the three things mentioned above,

and which king William put in practice, the compounding
with France, to prevent if possible a war, in which we were
averse to engage?

Allow me to push these reflections a little further, and to
observe to your lordship, that if the proposal of sending the
archduke into Spain had been accepted in time by the
imperial court, and taken effect and become a measure of
the confederacy, that war indeed would have been protracted; but France could not have hindered the passage of
this prince and his German forces: and our fleet would have
been better employed in escorting them, and in covering
the coasts of Spain and of the dominions of that crown both
in Europe and in America, than it was in so many unmeaning
expeditions from the battle of La Hogue to the end of the
war. France indeed would have made her utmost efforts to
have had satisfaction on her pretensions, as ill founded as
they were. She would have ended that war, as we began the
next, when we demanded a reasonable satisfaction for the
emperor: and though I think that the allies would have had,
in very many respects, more advantages in defending
Spain, than in attacking France; yet, upon a supposition
that the defence would have been as ill-conducted as the
attack was, and that by consequence, whether Charles the
second had lived to the conclusion of this war, or had died
before it, the war must have ended in some partition or
other; this partition would have been made by the Spaniards
themselves. They had been forced to compound with
France on her former pretensions, and they must and they
would have compounded on these, with an Austrian
prince on the throne, just as they compounded, and probably
much better than they compounded, on the pretensions we
supported against them, when they had a prince of Bourbon

on their throne. France could not have distressed the Spaniards, nor have over-run their monarchy, if they had been united; and they would have been united in this case, and supported by the whole confederacy: as we distressed both France and them, over-run their monarchy in one hemisphere, and might have done so in both, when they were disunited, and supported by France alone. France would not have acted, in such negociations, the ridiculous part which the emperor acted in those that led to the peace of Utrecht, nor have made her bargain worse by neglecting to make it in time. But the war ending as it did, though I cannot see how king William could avoid leaving the crown of Spain and that entire monarchy at the discretion of Lewis the fourteenth, otherwise than by compounding to prevent a new war he was in no sort prepared to make; yet it is undeniable, that, by consenting to a partition of their monarchy, he threw the Spaniards into the arms of France. The first partition might have taken place, perhaps, if the electoral prince of Bavaria had lived, whom the French and Spaniards too would have seen much more willingly than the archduke on the throne of Spain. For among all the parties into which that court was divided in one thousand six hundred and ninety-eight, when this treaty was made, that of Austria was grown the weakest, by the disgust taken at a German queen, and at the rapacity and insolence of her favourites. The French were looked upon with esteem and kindness at Madrid; but the Germans were become, or growing to be, objects of contempt to the ministers, and of aversion to the people. The electoral prince died in one thousand six hundred and ninety-nine. The star of Austria, so fatal to all those who were obstacles to the ambition of that house, prevailed; as the elector expressed himself in the first pangs of his grief. The state of things changed very much by his death. The archduke was to have Spain and the Indies, according to a second partition: and the Spaniards, who had expressed great resentment at the first, were pushed beyond their bearing by this. They soon appeared to be so; for the second treaty of partition was signed in March one thousand seven hundred; and the will was made, to the best of my remembrance, in the October following. I shall not enter here into many particulars concerning these great events. They will be related faithfully, and I hope fully explained, in a work which your lordship may take the trouble very probably from perusing some time or other, and which I shall rather leave, than give to the public. Something however must be said more, to continue and wind up this summary of the latter period of modern history.

France then saw her advantage, and improved it no doubt, though not in the manner, nor with the circumstances, that some lying scribblers of memorials and anecdotes have advanced. She had sent one of the ablest men of her court to that of Madrid, the marshal of Harcourt, and she had stipulated in the second treaty of partition, that the archduke should go neither into Spain nor the dutchy of Milan, during the life of Charles the second. She was willing to have her option between a treaty and a will. By the acceptation of the will, all king William's measures were broke. He was unprepared for war as much as when he made these treaties to prevent one; and if he meant in making them, what some wise, but refining men have suspected, and what I confess I see no reason to believe, only to gain time by the difficulty of executing them, and to prepare for making war, whenever the death of the king

of Spain should alarm mankind, and rouse his own subjects
out of their inactivity and neglect of foreign interests: if so,
he was disappointed in that too; for France took possession
of the whole monarchy at once, and with universal concurrence, at least without opposition or difficulty, in favour
of the duke of Anjou. By what has been observed, or
hinted rather, very shortly, and I fear a little confusedly, it
is plain, that reducing the power of France, and securing
the whole Spanish succession to the house of Austria, were
two points that king William, at the head of the British
and Dutch commonwealths and of the greatest confederacy
Europe had seen, was obliged to give up. All the acquisitions that France cared to keep for the maintenance of her
power were confirmed to her by the treaty of Ryswic: and
king William allowed, indirectly at least, the pretensions of
the house of Bourbon to the Spanish succession, as Lewis
the fourteenth allowed, in the same manner, those of the
house of Austria, by the treaties of partition. Strange
situation! in which no expedient remained to prepare for an
event, visibly so near, and of such vast importance as the
death of the king of Spain, but a partition of his monarchy,
without his consent, or his knowledge! If king William
had not made this partition, the emperor would have made
one, and with as little regard to trade, to the barrier of the
seven provinces, or to the general system of Europe, as had
been shewed by him when he made the private treaty with
France already mentioned, in one thousand six hundred and
sixty-eight. The ministers of Vienna were not wanting to
insinuate to those of France overtures of a separate treaty,
as more conducive to their common interests than the
accession of his imperial majesty to that of partition. But
the councils of Versailles judged very reasonably, that a

partition made with England and Holland would be more effectual than any other, if a partition was to take place: and that such a partition would be just as effectual as one made with the emperor, to furnish arguments to the emissaries of France, and motives to the Spanish councils, if a will in favour of France could be obtained. I repeat it again; I cannot see what king William could do in such circumstances as he found himself in after thirty years struggle, except what he did: neither can I see how he could do what he did, especially after the resentment expressed by the Spaniards, and the furious memorial presented by Canales on the conclusion of the first treaty of partition, without apprehending that the consequence would be a will in favour of France. He was in the worst of all political circumstances, and that wherein no one good measure remains to be taken; and out of which he left the two nations, at the head of whom he had been so long, to fight and negociate themselves and their confederates, as well as they could.

When this will was made and accepted, Lewis the fourteenth had succeeded, and the powers in opposition to him had failed, in all the great objects of interest and ambition, which they had kept in sight for more than forty years; that is, from the beginning of the present period. The actors changed their parts in the tragedy that followed. The power, that had so long and so cruelly attacked, was now to defend, the Spanish monarchy: and the powers, that had so long defended, were now to attack it. Let us see how this was brought about: and that we may see it the better, and make a better judgment of all that passed from the death of Charles the second to the peace of Utrecht, let us go back to the time of his death, and consider the circumstances that formed this complicated state of affairs in three views; a view of right, a view of policy, and a view of power.

The right of succeeding to the crown of Spain would have been undoubtedly in the children of Maria Theresa, that is, in the house of Bourbon; if this right had not been barred by the solemn renunciations so often mentioned. The pretensions of the house of Austria were founded on these renunciations, on the ratification of them by the Pyrenean treaty, and the confirmation of them by the will of Philip the fourth. The pretensions of the house of Bourbon were founded on a supposition, it was indeed no more, and a vain one too, that these renunciations were in their nature null. On this foot the dispute of right stood during the life of Charles the second, and on the same it would have continued to stand even after his death, if the renunciations had remained unshaken; if his will, like that of his father, had confirmed them, and had left the crown, in pursuance of them, to the house of Austria. But the will of Charles the second, annulling these renunciations, took away the sole foundation of the Austrian pretensions; for, however this act might be obtained, it was just as valid as his father's, and was confirmed by the universal concurrence of the Spanish nation to the new settlement he made of that crown. Let it be, as I think it ought to be, granted, that the true heirs could not claim against renunciations that were, if I may say so, conditions of their birth: but Charles the second had certainly as good a right to change the course of succession agreeable to the order of nature and the constitution of that monarchy, after his true heirs were born, as Philip the fourth had to change it, contrary to this order and this constitution, before they were born, or at any other time. He had as good a right, in short, to dispense with the Pyrenean treaty, and to set it aside in this respect, as his father had to make it: so that the renunciations being annulled by that party to the Pyrenean treaty who had exacted them, they could be deemed no longer binding, by virtue of this treaty, on the party who had made them. The sole question that remained therefore between these rival houses, as to right, was this, whether the engagements taken by Lewis the fourteenth in the partition-treaties obliged him to adhere to the terms of the last of them in all events, and to deprive his family of the succession, which the king of Spain opened, and the Spanish nation offered to them; rather than to depart from a composition he had made, on pretensions that were disputable then, but were now out of dispute? It may be said, and it was said, that the treaties of partition being absolute, without any condition or exception relative to any disposition the king of Spain had made, or might make of his succession, in favour of Bourbon or Austria; the disposition made by his will, in favour of the duke of Anjou, could not affect the engagements so lately taken by Lewis the fourteenth in these treaties, nor dispense with a literal observation of them. This might be true on strict principles of justice; but I apprehend that none of these powers who exclaimed so loudly against the perfidy of France in this case, would have been more scrupulous in a parallel case. The maxim 'summum jus est summa injuria' would have been quoted, and the rigid letter of treaties would have been softened by an equitable interpretation of their spirit and intention. His imperial majesty, above all, had not the least colour of right to exclaim against France on this occasion; for in general, if his family was to be stripped of all the dominions they have acquired by breach of faith, and means much worse than the acceptation of the will, even allowing all the invidious circumstances imputed to the conduct of France to be true, the Austrian family would sink from their present grandeur to that low state they were in two or three centuries ago. In particular, the emperor, who had constantly refused to accede to the treaties of partition, or to submit to the dispositions made by them, had not the least plausible pretence to object to Lewis the fourteenth, that he departed from them. Thus, I think, the right of the two houses stood on the death of Charles the second. The right of the Spaniards, an independent nation, to regulate their own succession, or to receive the prince whom the dying monarch had called to it; and the right of England and Holland to regulate the succession, to divide, and parcel out this monarchy in different lots, it would be equally foolish to go about to establish. One is too evident, the other too absurd, to admit of any proof. But enough has been said concerning right, which was in truth little regarded by any of the parties concerned immediately or remotely in the whole course of these proceedings. Particular interests were alone regarded, and these were pursued as ambition, fear, resentment, and vanity directed: I mean the ambition of the two houses contending for superiority of power; the fear of England and Holland, lest this superiority should become too great in either; the resentment of Spain at the dismemberment of that monarchy projected by the partition-treaties; and the vanity of that nation, as well as the princes of the house of Bourbon: for as vanity mingled with resentment to make the will, vanity had a great share in determining the acceptation of it.

Let us now consider the same conjuncture in a view of policy. The policy of the Spanish councils was this. They

could not brook that their monarchy should be divided:
and this principle is expressed strongly in the will of Charles
the second, where he exhorts his subjects not to suffer any
dismemberment or diminution of a monarchy founded by his
predecessors with so much glory. Too weak to hinder this
dismemberment by their own strength, too well apprised of
the little force and little views of the court of Vienna, and
their old allies having engaged to procure this dismemberment even by force of arms; nothing remained for them to
do, upon this principle, but to detach France from the
engagements of the partition-treaties, by giving their whole
monarchy to a prince of the house of Bourbon. As much as
may have been said concerning the negociations of France
to obtain a will in her favour, and yet to keep in reserve the
advantages stipulated for her by the partition-treaties, if such
a will could not be obtained, and though I am persuaded
that the marshal of Harcourt, who helped to procure this
will, made his court to Lewis the fourteenth as much as the
marshal of Tallard, who negociated the partitions; yet it is
certain, that the acceptation of the will was not a measure
definitely taken at Versailles when the king of Spain died.
The alternative divided those councils, and, without
entering at this time into the arguments urged on each side,
adhering to the partitions seemed the cause of France,
accepting the will that of the house of Bourbon.

It has been said by men of great weight in the councils of
Spain, and was said at that time by men as little fond of the
house of Bourbon, or of the French nation, as their fathers
had been; that if England and Holland had not formed a
confederacy and begun a war, they would have made
Philip the fifth as good a Spaniard as any of the preceding
Philips, and not have endured the influence of French

councils in the administration of their government: but that we threw them entirely into the hands of France when we began the war, because the fleets and armies of this crown being necessary to their defence, they could not avoid submitting to this influence as long as the same necessity continued; and, in fact, we have seen that the influence lasted no longer. But notwithstanding this, it must be confessed, that a war was unavoidable. The immediate securing of commerce and of barriers, the preventing an union of the two monarchies in some future time, and the preservation of a certain degree at least of equality in the scales of power, were points too important to England, Holland, and the rest of Europe, to be rested on the moderation of French, and the vigour of Spanish councils, under a prince of the house of France. If satisfaction to the house of Austria, to whose rights England and Holland shewed no great regard whilst they were better founded than they were since the will, had been alone concerned; a drop of blood spilt, or five shillings spent in the quarrel, would have been too much profusion. But this was properly the scale into which it became the common interest to throw all the weight that could be taken out of that of Bourbon. And therefore your lordship will find, that when negociations with d'Avaux were set on foot in Holland to prevent a war, or rather on our part to gain time to prepare for it, in which view the Dutch and we had both acknowledged Philip king of Spain; the great article we insisted on was, that reasonable satisfaction should be given the emperor, upon his pretensions founded on the treaty of partition. We could do no otherwise; and France who offered to make the treaty of Ryswic the foundation of that treaty, could do no otherwise than refuse to consent that the treaty of partition should be so, after accepting the will, and thereby engaging to oppose all partition or dismemberment of the Spanish monarchy. I should mention none of the other demands of England and Holland, if I could neglect to point out to your lordship's observation, that the same artifice was employed at this time, to perplex the more a negociation that could not succeed on other accounts, as we saw employed in the course of the war, by the English and Dutch ministers, to prevent the success of negociations that might and ought to have succeeded. The demand I mean, is that of "a liberty not only to explain the terms proposed, but to increase or amplify them in the course of the negociation." I do not remember the words, but this is the sense, and this was the meaning of the confederates in both cases.

In the former, king William was determined to begin the war by all the rules of good policy; since he could not obtain, nay since France could not grant in that conjuncture, nor without being forced to it by a war, what he was obliged by these very rules to demand. He intended therefore nothing by this negociation, if it may be called such, but to preserve forms and appearances, and perhaps, which many have suspected, to have time to prepare, as I hinted just now, both abroad and at home. Many things concurred to favour his preparations abroad. The alarm, that had been given by the acceptation of the will, was increased by every step that France made to secure the effect of it. Thus, for instance, the suprising and seizing the Dutch troops, in the same night, and at the same hour, that were dispersed in the garrisons of the Spanish Netherlands, was not excused by the necessity of securing those places to the obedience of Philip, nor softened by the immediate dismission of those troops. The impression it made was much the same as those of the surprises and seizures of France in former usurpations. No one knew then, that the sovereignty of the ten provinces was to be yielded up to the elector of Bavaria: and every one saw that there remained no longer any barrier between France and the seven provinces. At home, the disposition of the nation was absolutely turned to a war with France, on the death of king James the second, by the acknowledgment Lewis the fourteenth made of his son as king of England. I know what has been said in excuse for this measure, taken as I believe, on Female importunity; but certainly without any regard to public faith, to the true interest of France in those circumstances, or to the true interest of the prince thus acknowledged, in any. It was said, that the treaty of Ryswic obliging his most christian majesty only not to disturb king William in his possession, he might without any violation of it have acknowledged this prince as king of England; according to the political casuistry of the French, and the example of France, who finds no fault with the powers that treat with the kings of England, although the kings of England retain the title of kings of France; as well as the example of Spain, who makes no complaints that other states treat with the kings of France, although the kings of France retain the title of Navarre. But besides, that the examples are not apposite, because no other powers acknowledge in form the king of England to be king of France, nor the king of France, to be king of Navarre; with what face could the French excuse this measure? Could they excuse it by urging that they adhered to the strict letter of one article of the treaty of Ryswic, against the plain meaning of that very article, and against the whole tenor of that treaty: in the same breath with which they justified the acceptation of the will, by pretending they adhered to the supposed spirit and general intention of the treaties of partition, in contradiction to the letter, to the specific engagements, and to the whole purport of those treaties? This part of the conduct of Lewis the fourteenth may appear justly the more surprising, because in most other parts of his conduct at the same time, and in some to his disadvantage, he acted cautiously, endeavoured to calm the minds of his neighbours, to reconcile Europe to his grandson's elevation, and to avoid all shew of beginning hostilities.

Though king William was determined to engage in a war with France and Spain, yet the same good policy that determined him to engage, determined him not to engage too deeply. The engagement taken in the grand alliance of one thousand seven hundred and one is, "To procure an equitable and reasonable satisfaction to his imperial majesty for his pretension to the Spanish succession; and sufficient security to the king of England, and the States General, for their dominions, and for the navigation and commerce of their subjects, and to prevent the union of the two monarchies of France and Spain." As king of England, as stateholder of Holland, he neither could nor did engage any further. It may be disputed perhaps among speculative politicians, whether the balance of power in Europe would have been better preserved by that scheme of partition, which the treaties, and particularly the last of them, proposed, or by that which the grand alliance proposed to be the object of the war? I think there is little room for such a dispute, as I shall have occasion to say hereafter more expresly. In this place I shall only say, that the object of this war, which king William meditated, and queen Anne waged, was a partition, by which a prince of the house of

Bourbon, already acknowledged by us and the Dutch as king of Spain, was to be left on the throne of that dismembered monarchy. The wisdom of those councils saw that the peace of Europe might be restored, and secured on this foot, and that the liberties of Europe would be in no danger.

The scales of the balance of power will never be exactly poized, nor in the precise point of equality either discernible or necessary to be discerned. It is sufficient in this, as in other human affairs, that the deviation be not too great. Some there will always be. A constant attention to these deviations is therefore necessary. When they are little their increase may be easily prevented by early care and the precautions that good policy suggests. But when they become great for want of this care and these precautions, or by the force of unforeseen events, more vigour is to be exerted, and greater efforts to be made. But even in such cases, much reflection is necessary on all the circumstances that form the conjuncture; lest, by attacking with ill success, the deviation be confirmed, and the power that is deemed already exorbitant become more so; and lest, by attacking with good success, whilst one scale is pillaged, too much weight of power be thrown into the other. In such cases, he who has considered, in the histories of former ages, the strange revolutions that time produces, and the perpetual flux and reflux of public as well as private fortunes, of kingdoms and states as well as of those who govern or are governed in them, will incline to think, that if the scales can be brought back by a war, nearly, though not exactly, to the point they were at before this great deviation from it, the rest may be left to accidents, and to the use that good policy is able to make of them.

When Charles the fifth was at the heighth of his power, and in the zenith of his glory, when a king of France and a pope were at once his prisoners; it must be allowed, that, his situation and that of his neighbours compared, they had as much at least to fear from him and from the house of Austria, as the neighbours of Lewis the fourteenth had to fear from him and from the house of Bourbon, when, after all his other success, one of his grandchildren was placed on the Spanish throne. And yet among all the conditions of the several leagues against Charles the fifth, I do not remember that it was ever stipulated, that "no peace should be made with him as long as he continued to be emperor and king of Spain; nor as long as any Austrian prince continued capable of uniting on his head the Imperial and Spanish crowns."

If your lordship makes the application, you will find that the difference of some circumstances does not hinder this example from being very apposite, and strong to the present purpose. Charles the fifth was emperor and king of Spain; but neither was Lewis the fourteenth king of Spain, nor Philip the fifth king of France. That had happened in one instance, which it was apprehended might happen in the other. It had happened, and it was reasonably to be apprehended that it might happen again, and that the Imperial and Spanish crowns might continue, not only in the same family, but on the same heads; for measures were taken to secure the succession of both to Philip the son of Charles. We do not find however that any confederacy was formed, any engagement taken, or any war made, to remove or prevent this great evil. The princes and states of Europe contented themselves to oppose the designs of Charles the fifth, and to check the growth of his power occasionally, and as interest invited, or necessity forced them to do; not constantly. They did perhaps too little against him, and sometimes too much for him: but if they did too little of one kind, time and accident did the rest. Distinct dominions, and different pretensions, created contrary interests in the house of Austria: and on the abdication of Charles the fifth, his brother succeeded, not his son, to the empire. The house of Austria divided into a German and a Spanish branch: and if the two branches came to have a mutual influence on one another, and frequently a common interest, it was not till one of them had fallen from grandeur, and till the other was rather aiming at it, than in possession of it. In short, Philip was excluded from the imperial throne by so natural a progression of causes and effects, arising not only in Germany but in his own family, that if a treaty had been made to exclude him from it in favour of Ferdinand, such a treaty might have been said very probably to have executed itself.

The precaution I have mentioned, and that was neglected in this case without any detriment to the common cause of Europe, was not neglected in the grand alliance of one thousand seven hundred and one. For in that, one of the ends proposed by the war, is to obtain an effectual security against the contingent union of the crowns of France and Spain. The will of Charles the second provides against the same contingency: and this great principle of preventing too much dominion and power from falling to the lot of either of the families of Bourbon or Austria, seemed to be agreed on all sides; since in the partition-treaty the same precaution was taken against an union of the Imperial and Spanish crowns. King William was enough piqued against France. His ancient prejudices were strong and well founded. He had been worsted in war, over-reached in negociation, and personally affronted by her. England and Holland were sufficiently alarmed and animated, and a party was not wanting, even in our island, ready to approve any engagements he would have taken against France and Spain, and in favour of the house of Austria; though we were less concerned, by any national interest, than any other power that took part in the war, either then or afterwards. But this prince was far from taking a part beyond that which the particular interests of England and Holland, and the general interest of Europe, necessarily required. Pique must have no more a place than affection, in deliberations of this kind. To have engaged to dethrone Philip, out of resentment to Lewis the fourteenth, would have been a resolution worthy of Charles the twelfth, king of Sweden, who sacrificed his country, his people, and himself at last, to his revenge. To have engaged to conquer the Spanish monarchy for the house of Austria, or to go, in favour of that family, one step beyond those that were necessary to keep this house on a foot of rivalry with the other, would have been, as I have hinted, to act the part of a vassal, not of an ally. The former pawns his state, and ruins his subjects, for the interest of his superior lord, perhaps for his lord's humour, or his passion: the latter goes no further than his own interest carries him; nor makes war for those of another, nor even for his own, if they are remote and contingent, as if he fought pro aris et focis, for his religion, his liberty, and his property. Agreeably to these principles of good policy, we entered into the war that began on the death of Charles the second: but we soon departed from them, as I shall have occasion to observe in considering the state of things, at this remarkable juncture, in a view of strength.

Let me recall here what I have said somewhere else. They who are in the sinking scale of the balance of power do not easily, nor soon, come off from the habitual prejudices of superiority over their neighbours, nor from the confidence that such prejudices inspire. From the year one thousand six hundred and sixty-seven, to the end of that century, France had been constantly in arms, and her arms had been successful. She had sustained a war, without any confederates against the principal powers of Europe confederated against her, and had finished it with advantage on every side, just before the death of the king of Spain. She continued armed after the peace, by sea and land. She increased her forces, while other nations reduced theirs, and was ready to defend, or to invade her neighbours, whilst, their confederacy being dissolved, they were in no condition to invade her, and in a bad one to defend themselves. Spain and France had now one common cause. The electors of Bavaria and Cologn supported it in Germany, the duke of Savoy was an ally, the duke of Mantua a vassal of the two crowns in Italy. In a word, appearances were formidable on that side; and if a distrust of strength, on the side of the confederacy, had induced England and Holland to compound with France for a partition of the Spanish succession, there seemed to be still greater reason for this distrust after the acceptation of the will, the peaceable and ready submission, of the entire monarchy of Spain to Philip, and all the measures taken to secure him in this possession. Such appearances might well impose. They did so on many, and on none more than on the French themselves, who engaged with great confidence and spirit in the war; when they found it, as they might well expect it would be, unavoidable. The strength of France

however, though great, was not so great as the French
thought it, nor equal to the efforts they undertook to make.
Their engagement, to maintain the Spanish monarchy
entire under the dominion of Philip, exceeded their strength.
Our engagement, to procure some out-skirts of it for the
house of Austria, was not in the same disproportion to our
strength. If I speak positively on this occasion, yet I
cannot be accused of presumption; because, how disputable
soever these points might be when they were points of
political speculation, they are such no longer, and the
judgment I make is dictated to me by experience. France
threw herself into the sinking scale, when she accepted the
will. Her scale continued to sink during the whole course
of the war, and might have been kept by the peace as low
as the true interest of Europe required. What I remember
to have heard the duke of Marlborough say, before he
went to take on him the command of the army in the
Low Countries in one thousand seven hundred and two,
proved true. The French mis-reckoned very much, if they
made the same comparison between their troops and those
of their enemies, as they had made in precedent wars.
Those that had been opposed to them in the last, were raw
for the most part when it began, the British particularly:
but they had been disciplined, if I may say so, by their
defeats. They were grown to be veteran at the peace of
Ryswic, and though many had been disbanded, yet they
had been disbanded lately: so that even these were easily
formed anew, and the spirit that had been raised continued
in all. Supplies of men to recruit the armies were more
abundant on the side of the confederacy, than on that of the
two crowns: a necessary consequence of which it seemed to
be, that those of the former would grow better, and those of

the latter worse, in a long, extensive, and bloody war. I believe it proved so; and if my memory does not deceive me, the French were forced very early to send recruits to their armies, as they send slaves to their gallies. A comparison between those who were to direct their councils, and to conduct the armies on both sides, is a task it would become me little to undertake. The event shewed, that if France had had her Conde, her Turenne, or her Luxemburg, to oppose to the confederates: the confederates might have opposed to her, with equal confidence, their Eugene of Savoy, their Marlborough, or their Starenberg. But there is one observation I cannot forbear to make. The alliances were concluded, the quotas were settled, and the season for taking the field approached, when king William died. The event could not fail to occasion some consternation on one side, and to give some hopes on the other: for, notwithstanding the ill success with which he made war generally, he was looked upon as the sole centre of union that could keep together the great confederacy then forming: and how much the French feared, from his life, had appeared a few years before, in the extravagant and indecent joy they expressed on a false report of his death. A short time shewed how vain the fears of some and the hopes of others were. By his death, the duke of Marlborough was raised to the head of the army, and indeed of the confederacy: where he, a new, a private man, a subject, acquired by merit and by management a more deciding influence, than high birth, confirmed authority, and even the crown of Great Britain, had given to king William. Not only all the parts of that vast machine, the grand alliance, were kept more compact and entire; but a more rapid and vigorous motion was given to the whole: and, instead of languishing out disastrous campaigns, we saw every scene of the war full of action. All those wherein he appeared, and many of those wherein he was not then an actor, but abettor however of their action, were crowned with the most triumphant success. I take with pleasure this opportunity of doing justice to that great man, whose faults I knew, whose virtues I admired; and whose memory, as the greatest general, and as the greatest minister, that our country or perhaps any other has produced, I honour. But besides this, the observation I have made comes into my subject, since it serves to point out to your lordship the proof of what I said above, that France undertook too much, when she undertook to maintain the Spanish monarchy entire in the possession of Philip: and that we undertook no more than what was proportionable to our strength, when we undertook to weaken that monarchy by dismembering it, in the hands of a prince of the house of Bourbon, which we had been disabled by ill fortune and worse conduct to keep out of them. It may be said that the great success of the confederates against France proves that their generals were superior to her's, but not that their forces and their national strength were so; that with the same force with which she was beaten, she might have been victorious: that if she had been so, or if the success of the war had varied, or been less decisive against her in Germany, in the Low Countries, and in Italy, as it was in Spain, her strength would have appeared sufficient, and that of the confederacy insufficient. Many things may be urged to destroy this reasoning: I content myself with one. France could not long have made even the unsuccessful efforts she did make, if England and Holland had done what it is undeniable they had strength to do; if besides pillaging, I do not say conquering,

the Spanish West Indies, they had hindered the French
from going to the South Sea; as they did annually during the
whole course of the war without the least molestation, and
from whence they imported into France in that time as
much silver and gold as the whole species of that kingdom
amounted to. With this immense and constant supply of
wealth France was reduced in effect to bankruptcy before
the end of the war. How much sooner must she have been
so, if this supply had been kept from her? The confession
of France herself is on my side. She confessed her inability
to support what she had undertaken, when she sued for
peace as early as the year one thousand seven hundred and
six. She made her utmost efforts to answer the expectation
of the Spaniards, and to keep their monarchy entire.
When experience had made it evident that this was beyond
her power, she thought herself justified to the Spanish
nation, in consenting to a partition, and was ready to
conclude a peace with the allies on the principles of their
grand alliance. But as France seemed to flatter herself, till
experience made her desirous to abandon an enterprize that
exceeded her strength; you will find, my lord, that her
enemies began to flatter themselves in their turn, and to
form designs and take engagements that exceeded theirs.
Great Britain was drawn into these engagements little by
little; for I do not remember any parliamentary declaration
for continuing the war till Philip should be dethroned,
before the year one thousand seven hundred and six: and
then such a declaration was judged necessary to second the
resolution of our ministers and our allies, in departing from
the principles of the grand alliance, and in proposing not
only the reduction of the French, but the conquest of the
Spanish monarchy, as the objects of the war. This new plan

had taken place, and we had begun to act upon it two years before, when the treaty with Portugal was concluded, and the arch-duke Charles, now emperor, was sent into Portugal first, and into Catalonia afterwards, and was acknowledged and supported as king of Spain.

When your lordship peruses the anecdotes of the times here spoken of, and considers the course and events of the great war which broke out on the death of the king of Spain, Charles the second, and was ended by the treaties of Utrecht and Radstat; you will find, that in order to form a true judgment on the whole you must consider very attentively the great change made by the new plan that I have mentioned; and compare it with the plan of the grand alliance, relatively to the general interest of Europe, and the particular interest of your own country. It will not, because it cannot, be denied, that all the ends of the grand alliance might have been obtained by a peace in one thousand seven hundred and six. I need not recall the events of that, and of the precedent years of the war. Not only the arms of France had been defeated on every side; but the inward state of that kingdom was already more exhausted than it had ever been. She went on indeed, but she staggered and reeled under the burden of the war. Our condition, I speak of Great Britain, was not quite so bad; but the charge of the war increased annually upon us. It was evident that this charge must continue to increase, and it was no less evident that our nation was unable to bear it without falling soon into such distress, and contracting such debts, as we have seen and felt, and still feel. The Dutch neither restrained their trade, nor overloaded it with taxes. They soon altered the proportion of their quotas, and were deficient even after this alteration in them. But, however, it must be allowed that they exerted their whole strength; and they and we paid the whole charge of the war. Since therefore by such efforts as could not be continued any longer, without oppressing and impoverishing these nations to a degree that no interest, except that of their very being, nor any engagement of assisting an alliance *totis viribus* can require, France was reduced, and all the ends of the war were become attainable; it will be worth your lordship's while to consider why the true use was not made of the success of the confederates against France and Spain, and why a peace was not concluded in the fifth year of the war. When your lordship considers this, you will compare in your thoughts what the state of Europe would have been, and that of your own country might have been, if the plan of the grand alliance had been pursued: with the possible as well as certain, the contingent as well as necessary, consequences of changing this plan in the manner it was changed. You will be of opinion, I think, and it seems to me, after more than twenty years of recollection, re-examination, and reflection, that impartial posterity must be of the same opinion; you will be of opinion, I think, that the war was wise and just before the change, because necessary to maintain that equality among the powers of Europe, on which the public peace and common prosperity depends: and that it was unwise and unjust after this change, because unnecessary to this end, and directed to other and to contrary ends. You will be guided by undeniable facts to discover, through all the false colours which have been laid, and which deceived many at the time, that the war, after this change, became a war of passion, of ambition, of avarice, and of private interest; the private interest of particular persons and particular states; to which the general interest of Europe was sacrificed so entirely; that if the terms insisted on by the confederates had been granted, nay if even those which France was reduced to grant, in one thousand seven hundred and ten, had been accepted, such a new system of power would have been created as might have exposed the balance of this power to deviations, and the peace of Europe to troubles, not inferior to those that the war was designed, when it began, to prevent. Whilst you observe this in general, you will find particular occasion to lament the fate of Great Britain in the midst of triumphs that have been sounded so high. She had triumphed indeed to the year one thousand seven hundred and six inclusively: but what were her triumphs afterwards? what was her success after she proceeded on the new plan? I shall say something on that head immediately. Here let me only say, that the glory of taking towns, and winning battles, is to be measured by the utility that results from those victories. Victories, that bring honour to the arms, may bring shame to the councils, of a nation. To win a battle, to take a town, is the glory of a general, and of an army. Of this glory we had a very large share in the course of the war. But the glory of a nation is to proportion the ends she proposes, to her interest and her strength; the means she employs to the ends she proposes, and the vigour she exerts to both. Of this glory, I apprehend, we have had very little to boast, at any time, and particularly in the great conjuncture of which I am speaking. The reasons of ambition, avarice, and private interest, which engaged the princes and states of the confederacy to depart from the principles of the grand alliance, were no reasons for Great Britain. She neither expected nor desired any thing more than what she might have obtained by adhering to those principles. What hurried our nation then, with so much spirit and ardour, into those of the new plan? your lordship will answer this question to yourself, I believe, by the prejudices and rashness of party; by the influence that the first successes of the confederate arms gave to our ministers: and the popularity they gave, if I may say so, to the war; by ancient and fresh resentments, which the unjust and violent usurpations, in short the whole conduct of Lewis the fourteenth, for forty years together, his haughty treatment of other princes and states, and even the style of his court, had created; and to mention no more, by a notion groundless but prevalent, that he was and would be master as long as his grandson was king of Spain, and that there could be no effectual measure taken, though the grand alliance supposed that there might, to prevent a future union of the two monarchies, as long as a prince of the house of Bourbon sat on the Spanish throne. That such a notion should have prevailed, in the first confusion of thoughts which the death and will of Charles the second produced, among the generality of men, who saw the fleets and armies of France take possession of all the parts of the Spanish monarchy, is not to be wondered at by those that consider how ill the generality of mankind are informed, how incapable they are of judging; and yet how ready to pronounce judgment; in fine, how inconsiderately they follow one another in any popular opinion which the heads of party broach, or to which the first appearances of things have given occasion. But, even at this time, the councils of England and Holland did not entertain this notion. They acted on quite another, as might be shewn in many instances, if any other besides that of the grand alliance was necessary. When these councils therefore seemed to entertain this notion afterwards, and acted and took engagements to act upon it, we must conclude that they had other motives. They could not have these; for they knew, that as the Spaniards had been driven by the two treaties of partition to give their monarchy to a prince of the house of Bourbon, so they were driven into the arms of France by the war that we made to force a third upon them If we acted rightly on the principles of the grand alliance, they acted rightly on those of the will: and if we could not avoid making an offensive war, at the expence of forming and maintaining a vast confederacy, they could not avoid purchasing the protection and assistance of France in a defensive war, and especially in the beginning of it, according to what I have somewhere observed already, by yielding to the authority and admitting the influence of that court in all the affairs of their government. Our ministers knew therefore, that if any inference was to be drawn from the first part of this notion, it was for shortening, not prolonging, the war; for delivering the Spaniards as soon as possible from habits of union and intimacy with France; not for continuing them under the same necessity, till by length of time these habits should be confirmed. As to the latter part of this notion, they knew that it was false and silly. Garth, the best natured ingenious wild man I ever knew, might be in the right when he said, in some of his poems at that time,

> —*An Austrian prince alone,*
> *Is fit to nod upon a Spanish throne.*

The setting an Austrian prince upon it was, no doubt, the surest expedient to prevent an union of the two monarchies of France and Spain; just as setting a prince of the house of

Bourbon on that throne was the surest expedient to prevent
an union of the imperial and Spanish crowns. But it was
equally false to say, in either case, that this was the sole
expedient. It would be no paradox, but a proposition
easily proved, to advance, that if these unions had been
effectually provided against, the general interest of Europe
would have been little concerned whether Philip or Charles
had nodded at Madrid. It would be likewise no paradox to
say, that the contingency of uniting France and Spain under
the same prince appeared more remote, about the middle of
the last great war, when the dethronement of Philip in
favour of Charles was made a condition of peace sine qua
non, than the contingency of an union of the Imperial and
Spanish crowns. Nay, I know not whether it would be a
paradox to affirm, that the expedient that was taken, and
that was always obvious to be taken, of excluding Philip
and his race from the succession of France, by creating an
interest in all the other princes of the blood, and by consequence a party in France itself, for their exclusion, whenever the case should happen, was not in its nature more
effectual than any that could have been taken: and some
must have been taken, not only to exclude Charles from
the empire whenever the case should happen that happened
soon, the death of his brother Joseph without issue male,
but his posterity likewise in all future vacancies of the
imperial throne. The expedient that was taken against
Philip at the treaty of Utrecht, they who opposed the peace
attempted to ridicule, but some of them have had occasion
since that time to see, though the case has not happened,
how effectual it would have been if it had: and he who
should go about to ridicule it after our experience, would
only make himself ridiculous. Notwithstanding all this, he,

who transports himself back to that time, must acknowledge, that the confederated powers in general could not but be of Garth's mind, and think it more agreeable to the common interest of Europe, that a branch of Austria, than a branch of Bourbon, should gather the Spanish succession, and that the maritime powers, as they are called impertinently enough with respect to the superiority of Great Britain, might think it was for their particular interest to have a prince, dependant for some time at least on them, king of Spain, rather than a prince whose dependance, as long as he stood in any, must be naturally on France. I do not say, as some have done, a prince whose family was an old ally, rather than a prince whose family was an old enemy; because I lay no weight on the gratitude of princes, and am as much persuaded that an Austrian king of Spain would have made us returns of that sort in no other proportion than of his want of us, as I am, that Philip and his race will make no other returns of the same sort to France. If this affair had been entire, therefore on the death of the king of Spain; if we had made no partition, nor he any will, the whole monarchy of Spain would have been the prize to be fought for: and our wishes, and such efforts as we were able to make, in the most unprovided condition imaginable, must have been on the side of Austria. But it was far from being entire. A prince of the house of Austria might have been on the spot, before the king of Spain died, to gather his succession; but instead of this a prince of the house of Bourbon was there soon afterwards, and took possession of the whole monarchy, to which he had been called by the late king's will, and by the voice of the Spanish nation. The councils of England and Holland therefore preferred very wisely, by their engagements in the grand alliance, what was more practicable though less eligible, to what they deemed more eligible, but saw become by the course of events, if not absolutely impracticable, yet an enterprize of more length, more difficulty, and greater expence of blood and treasure, than these nations were able to bear; or than they ought to bear, when their security and that of the rest of Europe might be sufficiently provided for at a cheaper rate. If the confederates could not obtain, by the force of their arms, the ends of the war, laid down in the grand alliance, to what purpose would it be to stipulate for more? And if they were able to obtain these, it was evident that, whilst they dismembered the Spanish monarchy, they must reduce the power of France. This happened; the Low Countries were conquered; the French were driven out of Germany and Italy: and Lewis the fourteenth, who had so long and so lately set mankind at defiance, was reduced to sue for peace.

If it had been granted him in one thousand seven hundred and six, on what foot must it have been granted? The allies had already in their power all the states that were to compose the reasonable satisfaction for the emperor. I say, in their power: because though Naples and Sicily were not actually reduced at that time, yet the expulsion of the French out of Italy and the disposition of the people of those kingdoms, considered, it was plain the allies might reduce them when they pleased. The confederate arms were superior till then in Spain, and several provinces acknowledged Charles the third. If the rest had been yielded to him by treaty, all that the new plan required had been obtained. If the French would not yet have abandoned Philip, as we had found that the Castilians would not even when our army was at Madrid, all that the old plan, the plan of the grand alliance, required had been obtained; but still France and Spain had given nothing to purchase a peace, and they were in circumstances not to expect it without purchasing it. They would have purchased it, my lord: and France as well as Spain, would have contributed a larger share of the price, rather than continue the war, in her exhausted state. Such a treaty of peace would have been a third treaty of partition indeed, but vastly preferable to the two former. The great objection to the former was drawn from that considerable increase of dominion, which the crown of France, and not a branch of the house of Bourbon, acquired by them. I know what may be said speciously enough to persuade, that such an increase of dominion would not have augmented, but would rather have weakened the power of France, and what examples may be drawn from history to countenance such an opinion. I know likewise, that the compact figure of France, and the contiguity of all her provinces, make a very essential part of the force of her monarchy. Had the designs of Charles the eighth, Lewis the twelfth, Francis the first, and Henry the second, succeeded, the dominions of France would have been more extensive, and I believe the strength of her monarchy would have been less. I have sometimes thought that even the loss of the battle of St. Quentin, which obliged Henry the second to recall the duke of Guise with his army out of Italy, was in this respect no unhappy event. But the reasoning which is good, I think, when applied to those times, will not hold when applied to ours, and to the case I consider here; the state of France, the state of her neighbours, and the whole constitution of Europe being so extremely different. The objection therefore to the two treaties of partition had a real weight. The power of France, deemed already exorbitant, would have been increased by this accession of dominion, in the hands of Lewis the fourteenth: and the use he intended to make of it by keeping Italy and Spain in awe, appears in the article that gave him the ports on the Tuscan coasts, and the province of Guipuscoa. This king William might, and, I question not, did see; but that prince might think too, that for this very reason Lewis the fourteenth would adhere, in all events, to the treaty of partition: and that these consequences were more remote, and would be less dangerous, than those of making no partition at all. The partition, even the worst that might have been made, by a treaty of peace in one thousand seven hundred and six, would have been the very reverse of this. France would have been weakened, and her enemies strengthened, by her concessions on the side of the Low Countries, of Germany, and Savoy. If a prince of her royal family had remained in possession of Spain and the West Indies, no advantage would have accrued to her by it, and effectual bars would have been opposed to an union of the two monarchies. The house of Austria would have had a reasonable satisfaction for that shadow of right, which a former partition gave her. She had no other after the will of Charles the second; and this may be justly termed a shadow, since England, Holland, and France could confer no real right to the Spanish succession, nor to any part of it. She had declined acceding to that partition, before France departed from it, and would have preferred the Italian provinces, without Spain and the West Indies, to Spain and the West Indies without the Italian provinces. The Italian provinces would have fallen to her share by this partition. The particular demands of England and Holland would have suffered no difficulty, and those that we were obliged by treaty to make

for others would have been easy to adjust. Would not this
have been enough, my lord, for the public security, for the
common interest, and for the glory of our arms? To have
humbled and reduced, in five campaigns, a power that had
disturbed and insulted Europe almost forty years; to have
restored, in so short a time, the balance of power in Europe
to a sufficient point of equality, after it had been more than
fifty years, that is from the treaty of Westphalia, in a gradual
deviation from this point; in short, to have retrieved, in one
thousand seven hundred and six, a game that was become
desperate at the beginning of the century. To have done all
this before the war had exhausted our strength, was the
utmost sure that any man could desire who intended the
public good alone: and no honest reason ever was, nor
ever will be given, why the war was protracted any longer;
why we neither made peace after a short, vigorous, and
successful war, nor put it entirely out of the power of
France to continue at any rate a long one. I have said, and it
is true, that this had been entirely out of her power, if we
had given greater interruption to the commerce of Old and
New Spain, and if we had hindered France from importing
annually, from the year one thousand seven hundred and
two, such immense treasures as she did import by the
ships she sent, with the permission of Spain to the South
Sea. It has been advanced, and it is a common opinion, that
we were restrained by the jealousy of the Dutch from making
use of the liberty given by treaty to them and us, and which,
without his imperial majesty's leave, since we entered into
the war, we might have taken, of making conquests in the
Spanish West Indies. Be it so. But to go to the South
Seas, to trade there if we could, to pillage the West Indies
without making conquests if we could not, and, whether we

traded or whether we pillaged, to hinder the French from trading there; was a measure that would have given, one ought to think, no jealousy to the Dutch, who might, and it is to be supposed would, have taken their part in these expeditions; or if it had given them jealousy, what could they have replied, when a British minister had told them: 'That it little became them to find fault that we traded with, or pillaged the Spaniards in the West Indies to the detriment of our common enemy, whilst we connived at them who traded with this enemy to his and their great advantage, against our remonstrances, and in violation of the condition upon which we had given the first augmentation of our forces in the Low Countries?' We might have pursued this measure notwithstanding any engagement that we took by the treaty with Portugal, if I remember that treaty right: but instead of this, we wasted our forces, and squandered millions after millions in supporting our alliance with this crown, and in pursuing the chimerical project which was made the object of this alliance. I call it chimerical, because it was equally so, to expect a revolution in favour of Charles the third on the slender authority of such a trifler as the admiral of Castile; and, when this failed us, to hope to conquer Spain by the assistance of the Portuguese, and the revolt of the Catalans. Yet this was the foundation upon which the new plan of the war was built, and so many ruinous engagements were taken.

The particular motives of private men, as well as of princes and states, to protract the war, are partly known, and partly guessed, at this time. But whenever that time comes, and I am persuaded it will come, when their secret motives, their secret designs, and intrigues, can be laid open, I presume to say to your lordship that the most confused scene of iniquity, and folly, that it is possible to imagine, will appear. In the mean while, if your lordship considers only the treaty of barrier, as my lord Townshend signed it, without, nay in truth, against orders; for the duke of Marlborough, though joint plenipotentiary, did not: if you consider the famous preliminaries of one thousand seven hundred and nine, which we made a mock-shew of ratifying, though we knew that they would not be accepted; for so the marquis of Torcy had told the pensionary before he left the Hague, as the said marquis has assured me very often since that time: if you enquire into the anecdotes of Gertruydenburg, and if you consult other authentic papers that are extant, your lordship will see the policy of the new plan, I think, in this light. Though we had refused, before the war began, to enter into engagements for the conquest of Spain, yet as soon as it began, when the reason of things was still the same, for the success of our first campaign cannot be said to have altered it, we entered into these very engagements. By the treaty wherein we took these engagements first, Portugal was brought into the grand alliance; that is, she consented to employ her formidable forces against Philip, at the expence of England and Holland, provided we would debar ourselves from making any acquisitions, and the house of Austria promise, that she should acquire many important places in Spain, and an immense extent of country in America. By such bargains as this, the whole confederacy was formed, and held together. Such means were indeed effectual to multiply enemies to France and Spain; but a project so extensive and so difficult as to make many bargains of this kind necessary, and necessary for a great number of years, and for a very uncertain event, was a project into which, for this very reason, England and Holland should not have entered. It is worthy your observation, my lord, that these bad bargains would not have been continued, as they were almost to our immediate ruin, if the war had not been protracted under the pretended necessity of reducing the whole Spanish monarchy to the obedience of the house of Austria. Now, as no other confederate except Portugal was to receive his recompence by any dismemberment of dominions in Old or New Spain, the engagements we took to conquer this whole monarchy had no visible necessary cause, but the procuring the accession of this power, that was already neuter, to the grand alliance. This accession, as I have said before, served only to make us neglect immediate and certain advantages, for remote and uncertain hopes; and chuse to attempt the conquest of the Spanish nation at our own vast expence, whom we might have starved, and by starving reduced both the French and them, at their expence.

I called the necessity of reducing the whole Spanish monarchy to the obedience of the house of Austria, a pretended necessity: and pretended it was not real, without doubt. But I am apt to think your lordship may go further, and find some reasons to suspect, that the opinion itself of this necessity was not very real, in the minds of those who urged it: in the minds I would say of the able men among them; for that it was real in some of our zealous British politicians, I do them the justice to believe. Your lordship may find reasons to suspect perhaps, that this opinion was set up rather to occasion a diversion of the forces of France, and to furnish pretences for prolonging the war for other ends.

Before the year one thousand seven hundred and ten, the war was kept alive with alternate success in Spain; and it

may be said therefore, that the design of conquering this
kingdom continued, as well as the hopes of succeeding.
But why then did the States General refuse, in one thousand seven hundred and nine, to admit an article in the
barrier-treaty, by which they would have obliged themselves
to procure the whole Spanish monarchy to the house of
Austria, when that zealous politician my lord Townshend
pressed them to it? If their opinion of the necessity of
carrying on the war, till this point could be obtained, was
real; why did they risque the immense advantages given
them with so much profuse generosity by this treaty,
rather than consent to an engagement that was so conformable to their opinion?

After the year one thousand seven hundred and ten, it
will not be said, I presume, that the war could be supported
in Spain with any prospect of advantage on our side. We
had sufficiently experienced how little dependance could be
had on the vigour of the Portuguese; and how firmly the
Spanish nation in general, the Castilians in particular, were
attached to Philip. Our armies had been twice at Madrid,
this prince had been twice driven from the capital, his rival
had been there, none stirred in favour of the victorious, all
wished and acted for the vanquished. In short, the falshood
of all those lures, by which we had been enticed to make
war in Spain, had appeared sufficiently in one thousand
seven hundred and six; but was so grossly evident in one
thousand seven hundred and ten, that Mr. Craggs, who was
sent towards the end of that year by Mr. Stanhope into
England, on commissions which he executed with much
good sense, and much address, owned to me, that in Mr.
Stanhope's opinion, and he was not apt to despond of
success, especially in the execution of his own projects,

nothing could be done more in Spain, the general attachment of the people to Philip and their aversion to Charles
considered: that armies of twenty or thirty thousand men
might walk about that country till dooms-day, so he
expressed himself, without effect: that wherever they came,
the people would submit to Charles the third out of terror,
and, as soon as they were gone, proclaim Philip the fifth
again out of affection: that to conquer Spain required a
great army; and to keep it, a greater.

Was it possible, after this, to think in good earnest of
conquering Spain, and could they be in good earnest who
continued to hold the same language, and to insist on the
same measures? Could they be so in the following year,
when the emperor Joseph died? Charles was become then
the sole surviving male of the house of Austria, and succeeded to the empire as well as to all the hereditary dominions of that family. Could they be in earnest who
maintained, even in this conjuncture, that "no peace could
be safe, honourable, or lasting, so long as the kingdom of
Spain and the West Indies remained in the possession of
any branch of the house of Bourbon?" Did they mean that
Charles should be emperor and king of Spain? In this
project they would have had the allies against them. Did
they mean to call the duke of Savoy to the crown of Spain,
or to bestow it on some other prince? In this project they
would have had his Imperial majesty against them. In
either case, the confederacy would have been broken: and
how then would they have continued the war? Did they
mean nothing, or did they mean something more than they
owned; something more than to reduce the exorbitant
power of France, and to force the whole Spanish monarchy
out of the house of Bourbon?

Both these ends might have been obtained at Gertruydenberg. Why were they not obtained? Read the preliminaries of one thousand seven hundred and nine, which
were made the foundation of this treaty. Inform yourself
of what passed there, and observe what followed. Your
lordship will remain astonished. I remain so every time I
reflect upon them, though I saw these things at no very
great distance, even whilst they were in transaction; and
though I know most certainly, that France lost, two years
before, by the little skill and address of her principal[1]
minister, in answering overtures made during the siege of
Lisle by a principal person among the allies,[2] such an
opportunity, and such a correspondence, as would have
removed some of the obstacles that lay now in her way,
have prevented others, and have procured her peace. An
equivalent for the thirty-seventh article of the preliminaries,
that is, for the cession of Spain and the West Indies, was the
point to be discussed at Gertruydenberg. Naples and
Sicily, or even Naples and Sardinia would have contented
the French, at least they would have accepted them as the
equivalent. Buys and Vanderdussen, who treated with
them, reported this to the ministers of the allies: and it was
upon this occasion that the duke of Marlborough, as Buys
himself told me, took immediately the lead, and congratu-
lated the assembly on the near approach of a peace; said,
that since the French were in this disposition, it was time to
consider what further demands should be made upon them,
according to the liberty observed in the preliminaries; and
exhorted all the ministers of the allies to adjust their
several ulterior pretensions, and to prepare their demands.

This proceeding, and what followed, put me in mind of

[1] Chamillard.   [2] Marlborough.

that of the Romans with the Carthaginians. The former were resolved to consent to no peace till Carthage was laid in ruins. They set a treaty however on foot, at the request of their old enemy, imposed some terms, and referred them to their generals for the rest. Their generals pursued the same method, and, by reserving still a right of making ulterior demands, they reduced the Carthaginians at last to the necessity of abandoning their city, or of continuing the war after they had given up their arms, their machines, and their fleet, in hopes of peace.

France saw the snare, and resolved to run any risque rather than to be caught in it. We continued to demand, under pretence of securing the cession of Spain and the West Indies, that Lewis the fourteenth should take on him to dethrone his grandson in the space of two months; and if he did not effect it in that time, that we should be at liberty to renew the war without restoring the places that were to be put into our hands according to the preliminaries; which were the most important places France possessed on the side of the Low Countries. Lewis offered to abandon his grandson; and, if he could not prevail on him to resign, to furnish money to the allies, who might at the expence of France, force him to evacuate Spain. The proposition made by the allies had an air of inhumanity, and the rest of mankind might be shocked to see the grandfather obliged to make war on his grandson. But Lewis the fourteenth had treated mankind with too much inhumanity in his prosperous days, to have any reason to complain even of this proposition. His people indeed, who are apt to have great partiality for their kings, might pity his distress. This happened, and he found his account in it. Philip must have evacuated Spain, I think, notwithstanding his own ob-

stinacy, the spirit of his queen, and the resolute attachment
of the Spaniards, if his grandfather had insisted, and been in
earnest to force him. But if this expedient was, as it was,
odious, why did we prefer to continue the war against
France and Spain, rather than accept the other? Why did
we neglect the opportunity of reducing, effectually and
immediately, the exorbitant power of France, and of
rendering the conquest of Spain practicable? both which
might have been brought about, and consequently the
avowed ends· of the war might have been answered by
accepting the expedient that France offered. "France,"
it was said, "was not sincere: she meant nothing more than
to amuse, and divide." This reason was given at the time;
but some of those who gave it then, I have seen ashamed to
insist on it since. France was not in a condition to act the
part she had acted in former treaties: and her distress was
no bad pledge of her sincerity on this occasion. But there
was a better still. The strong places that she must have put
into the hands of the allies, would have exposed her, on the
least breach of faith, to see, not her frontier alone, but even
the provinces that lie behind it desolated: and prince
Eugene might have had the satisfaction, it is said, I know
not how truly, he desired, of marching with the torch in his
hand to Versailles.

Your lordship will observe, that the conferences at
Gertruydenberg ending in the manner they did, the in-
flexibility of the allies gave new life and spirit to the French
and Spanish nations, distressed and exhausted as they were.
The troops of the former withdrawn out of Spain, and the
Spaniards left to defend themselves as they could, the
Spaniards alone obliged us to retreat from Madrid, and
defeated us in our retreat. But your lordship may think

perhaps, as I do, that if Lewis the fourteenth had bound
himself by a solemn treaty to abandon his grandson, had
paid a subsidy to dethrone him, and had consented to
acknowledge another king of Spain, the Spaniards would
not have exerted the same zeal for Philip; the actions of
Almenara and Saragossa might have been decisive, and
those of Brihuegha and Villa Viciosa would not have
happened. After all these events, how could any reasonable
man expect that a war should be supported with advantage
in Spain, to which the court of Vienna had contributed
nothing from the first, scarce bread to their arch-duke;
which Portugal waged faintly and with deficient quotas;
and which the Dutch had in a manner renounced, by
neglecting to recruit their forces? How was Charles to be
placed on the Spanish throne, or Philip at least to be driven
out of it? by the success of the confederate arms in other
parts. But what success sufficient to this purpose, could we
expect? This question may be answered best, by shewing
what success we had.

Portugal and Savoy did nothing before the death of the
emperor Joseph; and declared in form, as soon as he was
dead, that they would carry on the war no longer to set the
crown of Spain on the head of Charles, since this would be
to fight against the very principle they had fought for. The
Rhine was a scene of inaction. The sole efforts, that were
to bring about the great event of dethroning Philip, were
those which the duke of Marlborough was able to make.
He took three towns in one thousand seven hundred and
ten, Aire, Bethune, and St. Venant: and one, Bouchain, in
one thousand seven hundred and eleven. Now this conquest being in fact the only one the confederates made that
year, Bouchain may be said properly and truly to have cost

our nation very near seven millions sterling; for your lordship will find, I believe, that the charge of the war for that year amounted to no less. It is true that the duke of Marlborough had proposed a very great project, by which incursions would have been made during the winter into France; the next campaign might have been opened early on our side; and several other great and obvious advantages might have been obtained; but the Dutch refused to contribute, even less than their proportion, for the queen had offered to take the deficiency on herself, to the expence of barracks and forage; and disappointed by their obstinacy the whole design.

We were then amused with visionary schemes of marching our whole army, in a year or two more, and after a town or two more were taken, directly to Paris, or at least into the heart of France. But was this so easy or so sure a game? The French expected we would play it. Their generals had visited the several posts they might take, when our army should enter France, to retard, to incommode, to distress us in our march, and even to make a decisive stand and to give us battle. I take what I say here from indisputable authority, that of the persons consulted and employed in preparing for this great distress. Had we been beaten, or had we been forced to retire towards our own frontier in the Low Countries, after penetrating into France, the hopes on which we protracted the war would have been disappointed, and, I think, the most sanguine would have then repented refusing the offers made at Gertruydenberg. But if we had beaten the French, for it was scarce lawful in those days of our presumption to suppose the contrary; would the whole monarchy of Spain have been our immediate and certain prize? Suppose, and I suppose it on good grounds, my lord, that the French had resolved to defend their country inch by inch, and that Lewis the fourteenth had determined to retire with his court to Lyons or elsewhere, and to defend the passage of the Loire, when he could no longer defend that of the Seine, rather than submit to the terms imposed on him: what should we have done in this case? Must we not have accepted such a peace as we had refused; or have protracted the war till we had conquered France first in order to conquer Spain afterwards? Did we hope for revolutions in France? We had hoped for them in Spain: and we should have been bubbles of our hopes in both. That there was a spirit raised against the government of Lewis the fourteenth, in his court, nay in his family, and that strange schemes of private ambition were formed and forming there, I cannot doubt: and some effects of this spirit produced perhaps the greatest mortifications that he suffered in the latter part of his reign.

A light instance of this spirit is all I will quote at this time. I supped, in the year one thousand seven hundred and fifteen, at a house in France where two[1] persons of no small figure, who had been in great company that night, arrived very late. The conversation turned on the events of the precedent war, and the negociations of the late peace, in the process of the conversation, one of them[2] broke loose, and said, directing his discourse to me, "Vous auriez pu nous écraser dans ce tems là: pourquoi ne l'avez-vous pas fait?" I answered him coolly, "Par ce que dans ce tems-là nous n'avons plus craint vôtre puissance." This anecdote, too trivial for history, may find its place in a letter, and may serve to confirm what I have admitted,

---

[1] The duke de La Feuillade and Mortemar.
[2] La Feuillade.

that there were persons even in France, who expected to
find their private account in the distress of their country.
But these persons were a few men of wild imaginations and
strong passions, more enterprizing than capable, and of
more name than credit. In general, the endeavours of
Lewis the fourteenth, and the sacrifices he offered to make
in order to obtain a peace, had attached his people more than
ever to him: and if Lewis had determined not to go farther
than he had offered at Gertruydenberg, in abandoning his
grandson, the French nation would not have abandoned
him.

But to resume what I have said or hinted already: the
necessary consequences of protracting the war in order
to dethrone Philip, from the year one thousand seven
hundred and eleven inclusively, could be no other than
these: our design of penetrating into France might have
been defeated, and have become fatal to us by a reverse
of fortune: our first success might not have obliged the
French to submit; and we might have had France to
conquer, after we had failed in our first attempt to conquer
Spain, and even in order to proceed to a second: the
French might have submitted, and the Spaniards not; and
whilst the former had been employed to force the latter,
according to the scheme of the allies; or whilst, the latter
submitting likewise, Philip had evacuated Spain, the high
allies might have gone together by the ears about dividing
the spoil, and disposing of the crown of Spain. To these
issues were things brought by protracting the war; by
refusing to make peace, on the principles of the grand
alliance at worst, in one thousand seven hundred and
six; and by refusing to grant it, even on those of the new
plan, in one thousand seven hundred and ten. Such con-

tingent events as I have mentioned stood in prospect before us. The end of the war was removed out of sight; and they, who clamoured rather than argued for the continuation of it, contented themselves to affirm, that France was not enough reduced, and that no peace ought to be made as long as a prince of the house of Bourbon remained on the Spanish throne. When they would think France enough reduced, it was impossible to guess. Whether they intended to join the Imperial and Spanish crowns on the head of Charles, who had declared his irrevocable resolution to continue the war till the conditions insisted upon at Gertruydenberg were obtained: whether they intended to bestow Spain and the Indies on some other prince: and how this great alteration in their own plan should be effected by common consent: how possession should be given to Charles, or to any other prince, not only of Spain but of all the Spanish dominions out of Europe, where the attachment to Philip was at least as strong as in Castile, and where it would not be so easy, the distance and extent of these dominions considered, to oblige the Spaniards to submit to another government: These points, and many more equally necessary to be determined, and equally difficult to prepare, were neither determined nor prepared; so that we were reduced to carry on the war, after the death of the emperor Joseph, without any positive scheme agreed to, as the scheme of the future peace, by the allies. That of the grand alliance we had long before renounced. That of the new plan was become ineligible; and, if it had been eligible, it would have been impracticable, because of the division it would have created among the allies themselves: several of whom would not have consented, notwithstanding his irrevocable resolution, that the emperor should be king of

Spain. I know not what part the protractors of the war, in
the depth of their policy, intended to take. Our nation had
contributed, and acted so long under the direction of their
councils, for the grandeur of the house of Austria, like one
of the hereditary kingdoms usurped by that family, that it
is lawful to think their intention might be to unite the
Imperial and Spanish crowns. But I rather think they had
no very determinate view, beyond that of continuing the war
as long as they could. The late lord Oxford told me, that
my lord Somers being pressed, I know not on what occasion
nor by whom, on the unnecessary and ruinous continuation
of the war; instead of giving reasons to shew the necessity
of it, contented himself to reply, that he had been bred up
in a hatred of France. This was a strange reply for a wise
man: and yet I know not whether he could have given a
better then, or whether any of his pupils could give a
better now.

The whig party in general acquired great and just
popularity, in the reign of our Charles the second, by the
clamour they raised against the conduct of that prince in
foreign affairs. They who succeeded to the name rather
than the principles of this party, after the revolution, and
who have had the administration of the government in their
hands with very little interruption ever since, pretending to
act on the same principle, have run into an extreme as
vicious and as contrary to all the rules of good policy, as
that which their predecessors exclaimed against. The old
whigs complained of the inglorious figure we made, whilst
our court was the bubble, and our king the pensioner of
France; and insisted that the growing ambition and power
of Lewis the fourteenth should be opposed in time. The
modern whigs boasted, and still boast, of the glorious

figure we made, whilst we reduced ourselves, by their councils, and under their administrations, to be the bubbles of our pensioners, that is of our allies; and whilst we measured our efforts in war, and the continuation of them, without any regard to the interest and abilities of our own country, without a just and sober regard, such an one as contemplates objects in their true light and sees them in their true magnitude, to the general system of power in Europe; and, in short, with a principal regard merely to particular interests at home and abroad. I say at home and abroad; because it is not less true, that they have sacrificed the wealth of their country to the forming and maintaining a party at home, than that they have done so to the forming and maintaining beyond all pretences of necessity, alliances abroad. These general assertions may be easily justified without having recourse to private anecdotes, as your lordship will find when you consider the whole series of our conduct in the two wars; in that which preceded, and that which succeeded immediately the beginning of the present century, but above all the last of them. In the administrations that preceded the revolution, trade had flourished, and our nation had grown opulent: but the general interest of Europe had been too much neglected by us; and slavery under the umbrage of prerogative, had been well-nigh established among us. In those that have followed, taxes upon taxes, and debts upon debts have been perpetually accumulated, till a small number of families have grown into immense wealth, and national beggary has been brought upon us; under the specious pretences of supporting a common cause against France, reducing her exorbitant power, and poising that of Europe more equally in the public balance: laudable designs no doubt, as far as they

were real, but such as, being converted into mere pretences,
have been productive of much evil; some of which we feel
and have long felt, and some will extend its consequences
to our latest posterity. The reign of prerogative was short:
and the evils and the dangers, to which we were exposed
by it, ended with it. But the reign of false and squandering
policy has lasted long, it lasts still, and will finally complete
our ruin. Beggary has been the consequence of slavery in
some countries: slavery will be probably the consequence of
beggary in ours; and if it is so, we know at whose door to
lay it. If we had finished the war in one thousand seven
hundred and six, we should have reconciled like a wise
people, our foreign and our domestic interests as nearly as
possible: we should have secured the former sufficiently,
and not have sacrificed the latter as entirely as we did by the
prosecution of the war afterwards. You will not be able
to see without astonishment, how the charge of the war
encreased yearly upon us from the beginning of it; nor
how immense a sum we paid in the course of it to supply
the deficiencies of our confederates. Your astonishment,
and indignation too, will encrease, when you come to
compare the progress that was made from the year one
thousand seven hundred and six exclusively, with the
expence of more than thirty millions, I do not exaggerate,
though I write upon memory, that this progress cost us, to
the year one thousand seven hundred and eleven inclusively.
Upon this view, your lordship will be persuaded that it was
high time to take the resolution of making peace, when the
queen thought fit to change her ministry, towards the end
of the year one thousand seven hundred and ten. It was
high time indeed to save our country from absolute in-
solvency and bankruptcy, by putting an end to a scheme of

conduct, which the prejudices of a party, the whimsy of some particular men, the private interest of more, and the ambition and avarice of our allies, who had been invited as it were to a scramble by the preliminaries of one thousand seven hundred and nine, alone maintained. The persons therefore, who came into power at this time, hearkened, and they did well to hearken, to the first overtures that were made them. The disposition of their enemies invited them to do so, but that of their friends, and that of a party at home who had nursed, and been nursed by the war, might have deterred them from it; for the difficulties and dangers, to which they must be exposed in carrying forward this great work, could escape none of them. In a letter to a friend it may be allowed me to say, that they did not escape me: and that I foresaw, as contingent but not improbable events, a good part of what has happened to me since. Though it was a duty therefore that we owed to our country, to deliver her from the necessity of bearing any longer so unequal a part in so unnecessary a war, yet was there some degree of merit in performing it. I think so strongly in this manner, I am so incorrigible, my lord, that if I could be placed in the same circumstances again, I would take the same resolution, and act the same part. Age and experience might enable me to act with more ability, and greater skill; but all I have suffered since the death of the queen should not hinder me from acting. Notwithstanding this, I shall not be surprized if you think that the peace of Utrecht was not answerable to the success of the war, nor to the efforts made in it. I think so myself, and have always owned, even when it was making and made, that I thought so. Since we had committed a successful folly, we ought to have reaped more advantage from it than we did: and, whether we had left Philip, or placed another prince on the throne of Spain, we ought to have reduced the power of France, and to have strengthened her neighbours, much more than we did. We ought to have reduced her power for generations to come, and not to have contented ourselves with a momentary reduction of it. France was exhausted to a great degree of men and money, and her government had no credit: but they, who took this for a sufficient reduction of her power, looked but a little way before them, and reasoned too superficially. Several such there were however; for as it has been said, that there is no extravagancy which some philosopher or other has not maintained, so your experience, young as you are, must have shewn you, that there is no absurd extreme, into which our party-politicians of Great Britain are not prone to fall, concerning the state and conduct of public affairs. But if France was exhausted: so were we, and so were the Dutch. Famine rendered her condition much more miserable than ours, at one time, in appearance and in reality too. But as soon as this accident, that had distressed the French and frightened Lewis the fourteenth to the utmost degree, and the immediate consequences of it were over; it was obvious to observe, though few made the observation, that whilst we were unable to raise in a year, by some millions at least, the expences of the year, the French were willing and able to bear the imposition of the tenth over and above all the other taxes that had been laid upon them. This observation had the weight it deserved; and sure it deserved to have some among those who made it, at the time spoken of, and who did not think that the war was to be continued as long as a parliament could be prevailed on to vote money. But supposing it to have deserved none, supposing the power of France to have been reduced as low as you please, with respect to her inward state; yet still I affirm, that such a reduction could not be permanent, and was not therefore sufficient. Whoever knows the nature of her government, the temper of her people, and the natural advantages she has in commerce over all the nations that surround her, knows that an arbitrary government, and the temper of her people enable her on particular occasions to throw off a load of debt much more easily, and with consequences much less to be feared, than any of her neighbours can: that although in the general course of things, trade be cramped, and industry vexed by this arbitrary government, yet neither one nor the other is oppressed; and the temper of the people, and the natural advantages of the country, are such, that how great soever her distress be at any point of time, twenty years of tranquility suffice to re-establish her affairs, and to enrich her again at the expence of all the nations of Europe. If any one doubts of this, let him consider the condition in which this kingdom was left by Lewis the fourteenth; the strange pranks the late duke of Orleans played, during his regency and administration, with the whole system of public revenue, and private property; and then let him tell himself, that the revenues of France, the tenth taken off, exceed all the expences of her government by many millions of livres already, and will exceed them by many more in another year.

Upon the whole matter, my lord, the low and exhausted state to which France was reduced, by the last great war, was but a momentary reduction of her power: and whatever real and more lasting reduction the treaty of Utrecht brought about in some instances, it was not sufficient. The power of France would not have appeared as great as it did, when England and Holland armed themselves and armed all Germany against her, if she had lain as open to the invasions of her enemies, as her enemies lay to her's. Her inward strength was great; but the strength of those frontiers which Lewis the fourteenth was almost forty years in forming, and which the folly of all his neighbours in their turns suffered him to form, made this strength as formidable as it became. The true reduction of the exorbitant power of France, I take no notice of chimerical projects about changing her government, consisted therefore in disarming her frontiers, and fortifying the barriers against her, by the cession and demolition of many more places than she yielded up at Utrecht; but not of more than she might have been obliged to sacrifice to her own immediate relief, and to the future security of her neighbours. That she was not obliged to make these sacrifices, I affirm was owing solely to those who opposed the peace: and I am willing to put my whole credit with your lordship, and the whole merits of a cause that has been so much contested, on this issue. I say a cause that has been so much contested; for in truth, I think it is no longer a doubt any where, except in British pamphlets, whether the conduct of those who neither declined treating, as was done in one thousand seven hundred and six; nor pretended to treat without a design of concluding, as was done in one thousand seven hundred and nine and ten, but carried the great work of the peace forward to its consummation; or the conduct of those who opposed this work in every step of its progress, saved the power of France from a greater and a sufficient reduction at the treaty of Utrecht. The very ministers, who were employed in this fatal opposition, are obliged to confess this truth. How should they deny it? Those of

Vienna may complain that the emperor had not the entire Spanish monarchy, or those of Holland that the States were not made masters directly and indirectly of the whole Low Countries. But neither they, nor any one else that has any sense of shame about him, can deny that the late queen, though she was resolved to retreat because she was resolved to finish the war, yet was to the utmost degree desirous to treat in a perfect union with her allies, and to procure them all the reasonable terms they could expect: and much better than those they reduced themselves to the necessity of accepting, by endeavouring to wrest the negociation out of her hands. The disunion of the allies gave France the advantages she improved. The sole question is, who caused this disunion? and that will be easily decided by every impartial man, who informs himself carefully of the public anecdotes of that time. If the private anecdotes were to be laid open as well as those, and I think it almost time they should, the whole monstrous scene would appear, and shock the eye of every honest man. I do not intend to descend into many particulars at this time: but whenever I, or any other person as well informed as I, shall descend into a full deduction of such particulars, it will become undeniably evident, that the most violent opposition imaginable, carried on by the Germans and the Dutch in league with a party in Britain, began as soon as the first overtures were made to the queen; before she had so much as begun to treat: and was therefore an opposition not to this or that plan of treaty, but in truth to all treaty; and especially to one wherein Great Britain took the lead, or was to have any particular advantage. That the Imperialists meant no treaty, unless a preliminary and impracticable condition of it was to set the crown of Spain on the emperor's head, will appear from this; that prince Eugene when he came into England, long after the death of Joseph and elevation of Charles, upon an errand most unworthy of so great a man, treated always on this supposition: and I remember with how much inward impatience I assisted at conferences held with him concerning quotas for renewing the war in Spain, in the very same room, at the cockpit, where the queen's ministers had been told in plain terms, a little before, by those of other allies, "that their masters would not consent that the Imperial and Spanish crowns should unite on the same head." That the Dutch were not averse to all treaty, but meant none wherein Great Britain was to have any particular advantage, will appear from this; that their minister declared himself ready and authorized to stop the opposition made to the queen's measures, by presenting a memorial, wherein he would declare, "that his masters entered into them, and were resolved not to continue the war for the recovery of Spain, provided the queen would consent that they should garrison Gibraltar and Port Mahon jointly with us, and share equally the Assiento, the South Sea ship, and whatever should be granted by the Spaniards to the queen and her subjects." That the whigs engaged in this league with foreign powers against their country, as well as their queen, and with a phrensy more unaccountable than that which made and maintained the solemn league and covenant formerly, will appear from this; that their attempts were directed not only to wrest the negociations out of the queen's hands, but to oblige their country to carry on the war, on the same unequal foot that had cost her already about twenty millions more than she ought to have contributed to it. For they not only continued to abet the emperor, whose inability to supply his

quota was confessed; but the Dutch likewise, after the
States had refused to ratify the treaty their minister
signed at London towards the end of the year one thousand
seven hundred and eleven, and by which the queen united
herself more closely than ever to them; engaging to pursue
the war, to conclude the peace, and to guarantee it, when
concluded, jointly with them; "provided they would keep
the engagements they had taken with her, and the conditions of proportionate expence under which our nation
had entered into the war." Upon such schemes as these was
the opposition to the treaty of Utrecht carried on: and the
means employed, and the means projected to be employed,
were worthy of such schemes; open, direct, and indecent
defiance of legal authority, secret conspiracies against the
state, and base machinations against particular men, who
had no other crime than that of endeavouring to conclude a
war, under the authority of the queen, which a party in the
nation endeavoured to prolong, against her authority. Had
the good policy of concluding the war been doubtful, it
was certainly as lawful for those, who thought it good, to
advise it, as it had been for those, who thought it bad, to
advise the contrary: and the decision of the sovereign on
the throne ought to have terminated the contest. But he
who had judged by the appearances of things on one side,
at that time, would have been apt to think, that putting an
end to the war, or to Magna Charta, was the same thing;
that the queen on the throne had no right to govern in-
dependently of her successor; nor any of her subjects a right
to administer the government under her, tho' called to it by
her, except those whom she had thought fit to lay aside.
Extravagant as these principles are, no other could justify
the conduct held at that time by those who opposed the

peace: and as I said just now, that the phrensy of this league was more unaccountable than that of the solemn league and covenant, I might have added, that it was not very many degrees less criminal. Some of those, who charged the queen's ministers, after her death, with imaginary treasons, had been guilty during her life of real treasons: and I can compare the folly and violence of the spirit that prevailed at that time, both before the conclusion of the peace, and, under pretence of danger to the succession after it, to nothing more nearly than to the folly and violence of the spirit that seized the tories soon after the accession of George the first. The latter indeed, which was provoked by unjust and impolitic persecution, broke out in open rebellion. The former might have done so, if the queen had lived a little longer. But to return.

The obstinate adherence of the Dutch to this league, in opposition to the queen, rendered the conferences of Utrecht, when they were opened, no better than mock conferences. Had the men who governed that commonwealth been wise and honest enough to unite, at least then cordially with the queen, and, since they could not hinder a congress, to act in concert with her in it; we should have been still in time to maintain a sufficient union among the allies, and a sufficient superiority over the French. All the specific demands that the former made, as well as the Dutch themselves, either to incumber the negociation, or to have in reserve according to the artifice usually employed on such occasions, certain points from which to depart in the course of it with advantage, would not have been obtained: but all the essential demands, all in particular that were really necessary to secure the barriers in the Low Countries and of the four circles against France, would have been so.

For France must have continued, in this case, rather to sue for peace, than to treat on an equal foot. The first dauphin, son of Lewis the fourteenth, died several months before this congress began: the second dauphin, his grandson, and the wife and the eldest son of this prince, died soon after it began, of the same unknown distemper, and were buried together in the same grave. Such family misfortunes following a long series of national misfortunes, made the old king, though he bore them with much seeming magnanimity, desirous to get out of the war at any tolerable rate, that he might not run the risque of leaving a child of five years old, the present king, engaged in it. The queen did all that was morally possible, except giving up her honour in the negociation, and the interest of her subjects in the conditions of peace, to procure this union with the States General. But all she could do was vain; and the same phrensy, that had hindered the Dutch from improving to their, and to the common advantage the public misfortunes of France, hindered them from improving to the same purposes the private misfortunes of the house of Bourbon. They continued to flatter themselves that they should force the queen out of her measures, by their intrigues with the party in Britain who opposed these measures, and even raise an insurrection against her. But these intrigues, and those of prince Eugene, were known and disappointed; and monsieur Buys had the mortification to be reproached with them publicly, when he came to take leave of the lords of the council, by the earl of Oxford; who entered into many particulars that could not be denied, of the private transactions of this sort, to which Buys had been a party, in compliance with his instructions, and, as I believe, much against his own sense and inclinations. As the season for taking the field advanced, the league proposed to defeat the success of the congress by the events of the campaign. But instead of defeating the success of the congress, the events of the campaign served only to turn this success in favour of France. At the beginning of the year, the queen and the States, in concert, might have given the law to friend and foe, with great advantage to the former; and with such a detriment to the latter, as the causes of the war rendered just, the events of it reasonable, and the objects of it neces- sary. At the end of the year, the allies were no longer in a state of giving, nor the French of receiving the law: and the Dutch had recourse to the queen's good offices, when they could oppose and durst insult her no longer. Even then, these offices were employed with zeal, and with some effect for them.

Thus the war ended, much more favourably to France than she expected, or they who put an end to it designed. The queen would have humbled and weakened this power. The allies who opposed her would have crushed it, and have raised another as exorbitant on the ruins of it. Neither one nor the other succeeded, and they who meant to ruin the French power preserved it, by opposing those who meant to reduce it.

Since I have mentioned the events of the year one thousand seven hundred and twelve, and the decisive turn they gave to the negociations in favour of France, give me leave to say something more on this subject. You will find that I shall do so with much impartiality. The disastrous events of this campaign in the Low Countries, and the consequences of them, have been imputed to the separation of the British troops from the army of the allies. The clamour against this measure was great at that time, and the prejudices which this clamour raised are great still among some men. But as clamour raised these prejudices, other prejudices gave birth to this clamour: and it is no wonder they should do so among persons bent on continuing the war; since I own very freely, that when the first step that led to this separation came to my knowledge, which was not an hour, by the way, before I wrote by the queen's order to the duke of Ormond, in the very words in which the order was advised and given, "that he should not engage in any siege, nor hazard a battle, till farther order," I was surprised and hurt. So much, that if I had had an opportunity of speaking in private to the queen, after I had received monsieur De Torcy's letter to me on the subject, and before she went into the council, I should have spoken to her, I think, in the first heat against it. The truth is, however, that the step was justifiable at that point of time in every respect, and therefore that the consequences are to be charged to the account of those who drew them on themselves, not to the account of the queen, nor of the minister who advised her. The step was justifiable to the allies surely, since the queen took no more upon her, no not so much by far, in making it, as many of them had done by suspending, or endangering, or defeating operations in the heat of the war, when they declined to send their troops, or delayed the march of them, or neglected the preparations they were obliged to make, on the most frivolous pretences. Your lordship will find in the course of your enquiries many particular instances of what is here pointed out in general. But I cannot help descending into some view of those that regard the emperor and the States General, who cried the loudest and with the most effect, though they had the least reason, on account of their own conduct, to com-

plain of the queen's. With what face could the emperor, for
instance, presume to complain of the orders sent to the
duke of Ormond? I say nothing of his deficiencies, which
were so great, that he had at this very time little more than
one regiment that could be said properly to act against
France and Spain at his sole charge; as I affirmed to prince
Eugene before the lords of the council, and demonstrated
upon paper the next day. I say nothing of all that preceded
the year one thousand seven hundred and seven, on which
I should have much to say. But I desire your lordship only
to consider, what you will find to have passed after the
famous year one thousand seven hundred and six. Was it
with the queen's approbation, or against her will, that the
emperor made the treaty for the evacuation of Lombardy,
and let out so great a number of French regiments time
enough to recruit themselves at home, to march into Spain,
and to destroy the British forces at Almanza? Was it with
her approbation, or against her will, that, instead of em-
ploying all his forces and all his endeavours, to make the
greatest design of the whole war, the enterprize on Toulon,
succeed, he detached twelve thousand men to reduce the
kingdom of Naples, that must have fallen of course? and
that an opportunity of ruining the whole maritime force of
France, and of ruining or subduing her provinces on that
side, was lost, merely by this unnecessary diversion, and
by the conduct of prince Eugene, which left no room to
doubt that he gave occasion to this fatal disappointment on
purpose, and in concert with the court of Vienna?

Turn your eyes, my lord, on the conduct of the States,
and you will find reason to be astonished at the arrogance of
the men who governed in them at this time, and who
presumed to exclaim against a queen of Great Britain, for

doing what their deputies had done more than once in that very country, and in the course of that very war. In the year one thousand seven hundred and twelve, at the latter end of a war, when conferences for treating a peace were opened, when the least sinister event in the field would take off from that superiority which the allies had in the congress, and when the past success of the war had already given them as much of this superiority as they wanted to obtain a safe, advantageous, honourable, and lasting peace, the queen directed her general to suspend till farther order the operations of her troops. In one thousand seven hundred and three, in the beginning of a war, when something was to be risqued or no success to be expected, and when the bad situation of affairs in Germany and Italy required, in a particular manner, that efforts should be made in the Low Countries, and that the war should not languish there whilst it was unsuccessful every where else; the duke of Marlborough determined to attack the French, but the Dutch deputies would not suffer their troops to go on: defeated his design in the very moment of it's execution, if I remember well, and gave no other reason for their proceeding than that which is a reason against every battle, the possibility of being beaten. The circumstance of proximity to their frontier was urged, I know, and it was said, that their provinces would be exposed to the incursions of the French if they lost the battle. But besides other answers to this vain pretence, it was obvious that they had ventured battles as near home as this would have been fought, and that the way to remove the enemy farther off was by action, not inaction. Upon the whole matter; the Dutch deputies stopped the progress of the confederate army at this time, by exercising an arbitrary and independent authority over the troops of the States. In one thousand seven hundred and five, when the success of the preceding campaign should have given them an entire confidence in the duke of Marlborough's conduct, when returning from the Moselle to the Low Countries he began to make himself and the common cause amends, for the disappointment which pique and jealousy in the prince of Baden, or usual sloth and negligence in the Germans, had occasioned just before, by forcing the French lines; when he was in the full pursuit of this advantage, and when he was marching to attack an enemy half defeated, and more than half dispirited; nay, when he had made his dispositions for attacking, and part of his troops had passed the Dyle—the deputies of the States once more tied up his hands, took from him an opportunity too fair to be lost; for these, I think, were some of the terms of his complaint: and in short the confederacy received an affront at least, where we might have obtained a victory. Let this that has been said serve as a specimen of the independency on the queen, her councils, and her generals, with which these powers acted in the course of the war; who were not ashamed to find fault that the queen, once, and at the latter end of it, presumed to suspend the operation of her troops till farther order. But be it that they foresaw what this farther order would be. They foresaw then, that as soon as Dunkirk should be put into the queen's hands, she would consent to a suspension of arms for two months, and invite them to do the same. Neither this foresight, nor the strong declaration which the bishop of Bristol made by the queen's order at Utrecht, and which shewed them that her resolution was not taken to submit to the league into which they had entered against her, could prevail on them to make a right use of these two months, by endeavouring to renew their union and good understanding with the queen; though I can say with the greatest truth, and they could not doubt of it at the time, that she would have gone more than half way to meet them, and that her ministers would have done their utmost to bring it about. Even then we might have resumed the superiority we began to lose in the congress; for, the queen and the States uniting, the principal allies would have united with them: and, in this case, it would have been so much the interest of France to avoid any chance of seeing the war renewed, that she must, and she would, have made sure of peace, during the suspension, on much worse terms for herself and for Spain, than she made it afterwards. But the prudent and sober States continued to act like froward children, or like men drunk with resentment and passion; and such will the conduct be of the wise governments in every circumstance, where a spirit of faction and of private interest prevails, among those who are at the head, over reason of state. After laying aside all decency in their behaviour towards the queen, they laid aside all caution for themselves. They declared "they would carry on the war without her." Landrecy seemed, in their esteem, of more importance than Dunkirk: and the opportunity of wasting some French provinces, or of putting the whole event of the war on the decision of another battle, preferable to the other measure that lay open to them; that I mean, of trying in good earnest, and in an honest concert with the queen during the suspension of arms, whether such terms of peace, as ought to satisfy them and the other allies, might not be imposed on France.

If the confederate army had broke into France, the campaign before this, or in any former campaign; and if the

Germans and the Dutch had exercised then the same inhumanity, as the French had exercised in their provinces in
former wars; if they had burnt Versailles, and even Paris,
and if they had disturbed the ashes of the dead princes that
repose at St. Denis, every good man would have felt the
horror, that such cruelties inspire: no man could have said
that the retaliation was unjust. But in one thousand seven
hundred and twelve, it was too late, in every respect, to
meditate such projects. If the French had been unprepared
to defend their frontier, either for want of means, or in a
vain confidence that the peace would be made, as our king
Charles the second was unprepared to defend his coast at
the latter end of his first war with Holland, the allies might
have played a sure game in satisfying their vengeance on the
French, as the Dutch did on us in one thousand six hundred
and sixty-seven; and imposing harder terms on them, than
those they offered, or would have accepted. But this was
not the case. The French army was, I believe, more numerous than the army of the allies, even before separation,
and certainly in a much better condition than two or three
years before, when a deluge of blood was spilt to dislodge
them, for we did no more, at Malplaquet. Would the Germans and the Dutch have found it more easy to force them
at this time, than it was at that? Would not the French
have fought with as much obstinacy to save Paris, as they
did to save Mons: and, with all the regard due to the duke
of Ormond and to prince Eugene, was the absence of the
duke of Marlborough of no consequence? Turn this affair
every way in your thoughts, my lord, and you will find
that the Germans and the Dutch had nothing in theirs,
but to break, at any rate, and at any risque, the negociations
that were begun, and to reduce Great Britain to the neces-

sity of continuing what she had been too long, a province
of the confederacy. A province indeed, and not one of the
best treated: since the confederates assumed a right of
obliging her to keep her pacts with them, and of dispensing
with their obligations to her, of exhausting her, without
rule, or proportion, or measure, in the support of a war, to
which she alone contributed more than all of them, and in
which she had no longer an immediate interest nor even
any remote interest that was not common, or, with respect
to her, very dubious; and, after all this, of complaining that
the queen presumed to hearken to overtures of peace, and to
set a negociation on foot, whilst their humour and ambition
required that the war should be prolonged for an indefinite
time, and for a purpose that was either bad or indeter-
minate.

The suspension of arms, that began in the Low Countries,
was continued, and extended afterwards by the act I
signed at Fontainebleau. The fortune of the war turned at
the same time: and all those disgraces followed, which
obliged the Dutch to treat, and to desire the assistance of
the queen, whom they had set at defiance so lately. This
assistance they had, as effectually as it could be given in the
circumstances, to which they had reduced themselves, and
the whole alliance: and the peace of Great Britain, Portugal,
Savoy, Prussia, and the States General, was made without
his imperial majesty's concurrence, in the spring of one
thousand seven hundred and thirteen; as it might have been
made, much more advantageously for them all, in that of
one thousand seven hundred and twelve. Less obstinacy on
the part of the States, and perhaps more decisive resolutions
on the part of the queen, would have wound up all these
divided threads in one, and have finished this great work

much sooner and better. I say, perhaps more decisive resolutions on the part of the queen; because, although I think that I should have conveyed her orders for signing a treaty of peace with France, before the armies took the field, much more willingly, than I executed them afterwards in signing that of the cessation of arms; yet I do not presume to decide, but shall desire your lordship to do so, on a review of all circumstances, some of which I shall just mention.

The league made for protracting the war having opposed the queen to the utmost of their power, and by means of every sort, from the first appearances of a negociation: the general effect of this violent opposition, on her and her ministers was, to make them proceed by slower and more cautious steps: the particular effect of it was, to oblige them to open the eyes of the nation, and to inflame the people with a desire of peace, by shewing, in the most public and solemn manner, how unequally we were burdened, and how unfairly we were treated by our allies. The first gave an air of diffidence and timidity to their conduct, which encouraged the league, and gave vigour to the opposition. The second irritated the Dutch particularly; for the emperor and the other allies had the modesty at least, not to pretend to bear any proportion in the expence of the war: and thus the two powers whose union was the most essential, were the most at variance, and the queen was obliged to act in a closer concert with her enemy who desired peace, than she would have done if her allies had been less obstinately bent to protract the war. During these transactions, my lord Oxford, who had his correspondencies apart, and a private thread of negociation always in his hands, entertained hopes that Philip would be brought to abandon Spain in favour of his father-in-law, and to content himself with the states of that prince, the kingdom of Sicily, and the preservation of his right of succession to the crown of France. Whether my lord had any particular reasons for entertaining these hopes, besides the general reasons founded on the condition of France, on that of the Bourbon family, and on the disposition of Lewis the fourteenth, I doubt very much. That Lewis, who sought, and had need of seeking peace, almost at any rate, and who saw that he could not obtain it, even of the queen, unless Philip abandoned immediately, the crown of Spain, or abandoned immediately, by renunciation and a solemn act of exclusion all pretension to that of France; that Lewis was desirous of the former, I cannot doubt. That Philip would have abandoned Spain with the equivalents that have been mentioned, or either of them, I believe likewise; if the present king of France had died, when his father, mother, and eldest brother did: for they all had the same distemper. But Lewis would use no violent means to force his grandson; the queen would not continue the war to force him; Philip was too obstinate, and his wife too ambitious, to quit the crown of Spain, when they had discovered our weakness, and felt their own strength in that country, by their success in the campaign of one thousand seven hundred and ten: after which my lord Stanhope himself was convinced that Spain could not be conquered, nor kept, if it was conquered, without a much greater army, than it was possible for us to send thither. In that situation it was wild to imagine, as the earl of Oxford imagined, or pretended to imagine, that they would quit the crown of Spain, for a remote and uncertain prospect of succeeding to that of France, and content themselves to be, in the mean time, princes of very small dominions. Philip therefore, after struggling long that he might not be obliged to make his option till the succession of France lay open to him, was obliged to make it, and made it, for Spain. Now this, my lord, was the very crisis of the negociation: and to this point I apply what I said above of the effect of more decisive resolutions on the part of the queen. It was plain, that if she made the campaign in concert with her allies, she could be no longer mistress of the negociations, nor have almost a chance for conducting them to the issue she proposed. Our ill success in the field would have rendered the French less tractable in the congress: our good success there would have rendered the allies so. On this principle, the queen suspended the operations of her troops, and then concluded the cessation.

Compare now the appearances and effect of this measure, with the appearances, and effect that another measure would have had. In order to arrive at any peace, it was necessary to do what the queen did, or to do more: and, in order to arrive at a good one, it was necessary to be prepared to carry on the war, as well as to make a shew of it; for she had the hard task upon her, of guarding against her allies, and her enemies both. But in that ferment, when few men considered any thing coolly, the conduct of her general, after he took the field, though he covered the allies in the siege of Quesnoy, corresponded ill, in appearance, with the declarations of carrying on the war vigorously that had been made, on several occasions, before the campaign opened. It had an air of double dealing; and as such it passed among those, who did not combine in their thoughts all the circumstances of the conjuncture, or who were infatuated with the notional necessity of continuing the

war. The clamour could not have been greater, if the queen
had signed her peace separately: and, I think, the appearances might have been explained as favourably in one case,
as in the other. From the death of the emperor Joseph, it
was neither our interest, nor the common interest, well
understood, to set the crown of Spain on the present
emperor's head. As soon therefore as Philip had made his
option, and if she had taken this resolution early, his
option would have been sooner made, I presume that the
queen might have declared that she would not continue the
war an hour longer to procure Spain for his Imperial
majesty; that the engagements, she had taken whilst he was
archduke, bound her no more; that, by his accession to the
empire, the very nature of them was altered; that she took
effectual measures to prevent, in any future time, an union
of the crowns of France and Spain, and, upon the same
principle, would not consent, much less fight, to bring
about an immediate union of the Imperial and Spanish
crowns; that they, who insisted to protract the war,
intended this union; that they could intend nothing else,
since they ventured to break with her, rather than to treat,
and were so eager to put the reasonable satisfaction, that
they might have in every other case, without hazard, on the
uncertain events of war; that she would not be imposed on
any longer in this manner; and that she had ordered her
ministers to sign her treaty with France, on the surrender
of Dunkirk into her hands; that she pretended not to
prescribe to her allies, but that she had insisted, in their
behalf, on certain conditions, that France was obliged to
grant to those of them, who should sign their treaties at the
same time as she did, or who should consent to an immediate cessation of arms, and during the cessation, treat

under her mediation. There had been more frankness, and more dignity in this proceeding, and the effect must have been more advantageous. France would have granted more for a separate peace, than for a cessation: and the Dutch would have been more influenced by the prospect of one, than of the other; especially since this proceeding would have been very different from theirs at Munster, and at Nimeghen, where they abandoned their allies, without any other pretence than the particular advantage they found in doing so. A suspension of the operations of the queen's troops, nay a cessation of arms between her and France, was not definitive; and they might, and they did, hope to drag her back under their, and the German yoke. This therefore was not sufficient to check their obstinacy, nor to hinder them from making all the unfortunate haste they did make to get themselves beaten at Denain. But they would possibly have laid aside their vain hopes, if they had seen the queen's ministers ready to sign her treaty of peace, and those of some principal allies ready to sign at the same time; in which case the mischief, that followed, had been prevented, and better terms of peace had been obtained for the confederacy: a prince of the house of Bourbon, who could never be king of France, would have sat on the Spanish throne, instead of an emperor; the Spanish scepter would have been weakened in the hands of one, and the Imperial scepter would have been strengthened in those of the other: France would have had no opportunity of recovering from former blows, nor of finishing a long unsuccessful war by two successful campaigns: her ambition, and her power, would have declined with her old king, and under the minority that followed: one of them at least might have been so reduced by the terms of peace, if the defeat of the allies in one thousand seven hundred and twelve, and the loss of so many towns as the French took in that and the following year, had been prevented, that the other would have been no longer formidable, even supposing it to have continued; whereas I suppose that the tranquillity of Europe is more due, at this time, to want of ambition, than to want of power, on the part of France. But, to carry the comparison of these two measures to the end, it may be supposed that the Dutch would have taken the same part, on the queen's declaring a separate peace, as they took on her declaring a cessation. The preparations for the campaign in the Low Countries were made; the Dutch like the other confederates, had a just confidence in their own troops, and an unjust contempt for those of the enemy; they were transported from their usual sobriety and caution by the ambitious prospect of large acquisitions, which had been opened artfully to them; the rest of the confederate army was composed of Imperial and German troops: so that the Dutch, the Imperialists, and the other Germans, having an interest to decide which was no longer the interest of the whole confederacy, they might have united against the queen in one case, as they did in the other; and the mischief that followed to them and the common cause, might not have been prevented. This might have been the case, no doubt. They might have flattered themselves that they should be able to break into France, and to force Philip, by the distress brought on his grandfather, to resign the crown of Spain to the emperor, even after Great Britain and Portugal, and Savoy too perhaps, were drawn out of the war: for these princes desired as little, as the queen, to see the Spanish crown on the emperor's head. But, even in this case, though the madness would have been greater, the effect would not have been worse. The queen would have been able to serve these confederates as well by being mediator in the negociations, as they left it in her power to do, by being a party in them: and Great Britain would have had the advantage of being delivered so much sooner from a burden, which whimsical and wicked politics had imposed, and continued upon her till it was become intolerable. Of these two measures, at the time when we might have taken either, there were persons who thought the last preferable to the former. But it never came into public debate. Indeed it never could; too much time having been lost in waiting for the option of Philip, and the suspension and cessation having been brought before the council rather as a measure taken, than a matter to be debated. If your lordship, or any one else, should judge, that, in such circumstances as those of the confederacy in the beginning of one thousand seven hundred and twelve, the latter measure ought to have been taken, and the gordian knot to have been cut, rather than to suffer a mock treaty to languish on, with so much advantage to the French as the disunion of the allies gave them; in short, if slowness, perplexity, inconsistency, and indecision should be objected, in some instances, to the queen's councils at that time; if it should be said particularly, that she did not observe the precise moment when the conduct of the league formed against her, being exposed to mankind, would have justified any part she should have taken (though she declared, soon after the moment was passed, that this conduct had set her free from all her engagements) and when she ought to have taken that of drawing, by one bold measure, her allies out of the war, or herself out of the confederacy, before she lost her influence on France: if all this should be objected, yet would the proofs brought to support these objections shew, that we were better allies than politicians; that the desire the queen had to treat in concert with her confederates, and the resolution she took not to sign without them, made her bear what no crowned head had ever borne before; and that where she erred she erred, principally by the patience, the compliance, and the condescension she exercised towards them, and towards her own subjects in league with them. Such objections as these may lie to the queen's conduct, in the course of this great affair; as well as objections of human infirmity to that of those persons employed by her in the transactions of it; from which neither those who preceded, nor those who succeeded, have, I presume, been free. But the principles on which they proceeded were honest, the means they used were lawful, and the event they proposed to bring about was just. Whereas the very foundation of all the opposition to the peace was laid in injustice and folly: for what could be more unjust, than the attempt of the Dutch and the Germans, to force the queen to continue a war for their private interest and ambition, the disproportionate expence of which oppressed the commerce of her subjects, and loaded them with debts for ages yet to come? a war, the object of which was so changed, that from the year one thousand seven hundred and eleven, she made it not only without any engagement, but against her own, and the common interest? What could be more foolish; you will think that I soften the term too much, and you will be in the right to think so: what could be more foolish, than the attempt of a party in Britain, to protract a war so ruinous to their country, without any reason that they durst avow, except that of wreaking the resentments of Europe on France, and that of uniting the Imperial and

Spanish crowns on an Austrian head? one of which was to purchase revenge at a price too dear; and the other was to expose the liberties of Europe to new dangers, by the conclusion of a war which had been made to assert and secure them.

I have dwelt the longer on the conduct of those who promoted, and of those who opposed, the negociations of the peace made at Utrecht, and on the comparison of the measure pursued by the queen with that which she might have pursued, because the great benefit we ought to reap from the study of history, cannot be reaped unless we accustom ourselves to compare the conduct of different governments, and different parties, in the same conjunctures, and to observe the measures they did pursue, and the measures they might have pursued, with the actual consequences that followed one, and the possible, or probable consequences, that might have followed the other; by this exercise of the mind, the study of history anticipates, as it were, experience, as I have observed in one of the first of these letters, and prepares us for action. If this consideration should not plead a sufficient excuse for my prolixity on this head, I have one more to add that may. A rage of warring possessed a party in our nation till the death of the late queen: a rage of negociating has possessed the same party of men, ever since. You have seen the consequences of one: you see actually those of the other. The rage of warring confirmed the beggary of our nation, which began as early as the revolution; but then it gave, in the last war, reputation to our arms, and our councils too. For though I think, and must always think, that the principle, on which we acted after departing from that laid down in the grand alliance of one thousand seven hundred and one, was wrong; yet must we confess that it was pursued wisely, as well as boldly. The rage of negociating has been a chargeable rage likewise, at least as chargeable in its proportion. Far from paying our debts, contracted in war, they continue much the same, after three and twenty years of peace. The taxes that oppress our mercantile interest the most are still in mortgage; and those that oppress the landed interest the most, instead of being laid on extraordinary occasions, are become the ordinary funds for the current service of every year. This is grievous, and the more so to any man, who has the honour of his country, as well as her prosperity at heart, because we have not, in this case, the airy consolation we had in the other. The rage of negociating began twenty years ago, under pretence of consummating the treaty of Utrecht: and, from that time to this, our ministers have been in one perpetual maze. They have made themselves and us, often, objects of aversion to the powers on the continent; and we are become at last objects of contempt, even to the Spaniards. What other effect could our absurd conduct have? What other return has it deserved? We came exhausted out of long wars; and, instead of pursuing the measures necessary to give us means and opportunity to repair our strength and to diminish our burdens, our ministers have acted, from that time to this, like men who sought pretences to keep the nation in the same exhausted condition, and under the same load of debt. This may have been their view perhaps; and we could not be surprised if we heard the same men declare national poverty necessary to support the present government, who have so frequently declared corruption and a standing army to be so. Your good sense, my lord, your virtue, and your love of your country, will always determine you to oppose such vile schemes, and to contribute your utmost towards the cure of both these kinds of rage; the rage of warring, without any proportionable interest of our own, for the ambition of others; and the rage of nego-ciating, on every occasion, at any rate, without a sufficient call to it, and without any part of that deciding influence which we ought to have. Our nation inhabits an island, and is one of the principal nations of Europe; but, to maintain this rank, we must take the advantages of this situation, which have been neglected by us for almost half a century; we must always remember that we are not part of the continent, but we must never forget that we are neighbours to it. I will conclude, by applying a rule, that Horace gives for the conduct of an epic or dramatic poem, to the part Great Britain ought to take in the affairs of the continent, if you allow me to transform Britannia into a male divinity, as the verse requires.

Nec Deus intersit, nisi dignus vindice nodus Inciderit.

If these reflections are just, and I should not have offered them to your lordship, had they not appeared both just and important to my best understanding, you will think that I have not spent your time unprofitably in making them, and exciting you by them to examine the true interest of your country relatively to foreign affairs; and to compare it with those principles of conduct, that I am persuaded, have no other foundation than party-designs, prejudices, and habits; the private interest of some men and the ignorance and rashness of others.

My letter is grown so long, that I shall say nothing to your lordship, at this time, concerning the study of modern history relatively to the interests of your country in domestic affairs; and I think there will be no need to do so at any other. The History of the rebellion by your great grandfather, and his private memorials, which your lordship has in manuscript, will guide you surely as far as they go: where they leave you, your lordship must not expect any history; for we have more reason to make this complaint, "abest enim historia literis nostris," than Tully had to put it into the mouth of Atticus, in his first book of laws. But where history leaves you, it is wanted least: the traditions of this century, and of the latter end of the last, are fresh. Many, who were actors in some of these events, are alive; and many who have conversed with those that were actors in others. The public is in possession of several collections and memorials, and several there are in private hands. You will want no materials to form true notions of transactions so recent. Even pamphlets, wrote on different sides and on different occasions in our party disputes, and histories of no more authority than pamphlets, will help you to come at truth. Read them with suspicion, my lord, for they deserve to be suspected: pay no regard to the epithets given, nor to the judgments passed; neglect all declamation, weigh the reasoning and advert to fact. With such precautions, even Burnet's history may be of some use. In a word, your lordship will want no help of mine to discover, by what progression the whole constitution of our country, and even the character of our nation, has been altered: nor how much a worse use, in a national sense, though a better in the sense of party politicks, the men called Whigs have made of long wars and new systems of revenue, since the revolution; than the men called Tories made, before it, of long peace, and stale prerogative. When you look back three or four generations ago, you will see that the English were a plain, perhaps a rough, but a good-natured hospitable people, jealous of their liberties, and able as well as ready to defend them, with their tongues, their pens, and their swords. The restoration began to turn hospitality into luxury, pleasure into debauch, and country peers and country commoners into courtiers and men of mode. But whilst our luxury was young, it was little more than elegance: the debauch of that age was enlivened with wit, and varnished over with gallantry. The courtiers and the men of mode knew what the constitution was, respected it, and often asserted it. Arts and sciences flourished, and, if we grew more trivial, we were not become either grossly ignorant, or openly profligate. Since the revolution, our kings have been reduced indeed to a seeming annual dependance on Parliament; but the business of parliament, which was esteemed in general a duty before, has been exercised in general as a trade since. The trade of parliament, and the trade of funds, have grown universal. Men, who stood forward in the world have attended to little else. The frequency of parliaments, that increased their importance, and should have increased the respect of them, has taken off from their dignity: and the spirit that prevailed, whilst the service in them was duty, has been debased since it became a trade. Few know, and scarce any respect, the British constitution: that of the Church has been long since derided; that of the State as long neglected; and both have been left at the mercy of the men in power, whoever those men were. Thus the Church, at least the hierarchy, however sacred in it's origin, or wise in it's institution, is become an useless burden on the State: and the State is become, under ancient and known forms, a new and un-definable monster; composed of a king without monarchical

splendour, a senate of nobles without aristocratical independency, and a senate of commons without democratical
freedom. In the mean time, my lord, the very idea of wit,
and all that can be called taste, has been lost among the
great; arts and sciences are scarce alive; luxury has been
increased but not refined; corruption has been established,
and is avowed. When governments are worn out, thus it is:
the decay appears in every instance. Public and private
virtue, public and private spirit, science and wit, decline all
together.

That you, my lord, may have a long and glorious share in
restoring all these, and in drawing our government back to
the true principles of it, I wish most heartily. Whatever
errors I may have committed in public life, I have always
loved my country: whatever faults may be objected to me
in private life, I have always loved my friend: whatever
usage I have received from my country, it shall never make
me break with her: whatever usage I have received from
my friends, I never shall break with one of them, while I
think him a friend to my country. These are the sentiments
of my heart. I know they are those of your lordship's:
and a communion of such sentiments is a tye that will
engage me to be, as long as I live,

My Lord,

Your most faithful servant.

For EU product safety concerns, contact us at Calle de José Abascal, 56–1°,
28003 Madrid, Spain or eugpsr@cambridge.org.